the Book of Bad

the Book of Bad

Stuff You Should Know Unless You're a Pussy

Christopher Lee Barish

Illustrated by Christian Kunze

REBEL BASE

REBEL BASE BOOKS
Citadel Press
Kensington Publishing Corp.
www.kensingtonbooks.com

REBEL BASE BOOKS are published by

Kensington Publishing Corp.
119 West 40th Street
New York, NY 10018

All Kensington titles, imprints, and distributed lines are available at special quantity discounts for bulk purchases for sales promotions, premiums, fund-raising, educational, or institutional use. Special book excerpts or customized printings can also be created to fit specific needs. For details, write or phone the office of the Kensington special sales manager: Kensington Publishing Corp., 119 West 40th Street, New York, NY 10018, attn: Special Sales Department; phone 1-800-221-2647.

This book contains information about illegal activity and substances. The publisher would like to emphasize that engaging in some of the activities in this book may carry heavy penalties and may threaten individual liberty or personal livelihood and may also cause serious injury. The aim of the publisher is to entertain and to educate. The publisher does not condone, in any way, the violation of law and does not wish to encourage readers to engage in any of the activities or techniques outlined in this book. In other words, "don't try this at home."

First printing: January 2011

10 9 8 7 6 5 4 3 2 1

Printed in the United States of America

Library of Congress Control Number: 2010931892

ISBN-13: 978-0-8065-3332-2
ISBN-10: 0-8065-3332-3

CONTENTS

ACKNOWLEDGMENTS

Much thanks to my family and friends for keeping their distance, and in some cases, completely disassociating themselves from me. I express my deepest gratitude to the world's scoundrels, deviants, and law enforcement for sharing their sacred knowledge in the ways of debauchery. Thanks to Andrea Somberg and Mike Shohl for knowing Bad when they saw it. To Richard Ember for his editing mastery. To Nona Sue for setting the tone. To Ken Friedman for his digital brilliance. To Suzanne Foley for her thorough research and fluid prose. And to Christian Kunze for lending his twisted talent to this project.

INTRODUCTION

Anyone who has an issue with this book can blame my step-sister. We had just arrived at Dulles International Airport in Washington, D.C., on a flight from Italy. At the baggage carousel, my step-sister noticed DEA agents with drug-sniffing dogs. She knelt down, slapped her knees and the dogs came huffing toward us. Unbeknownst to her, I had a couple of squares of hashish hidden in my sock, which I had purchased in Milan. I was terrified that the dogs would go wild at my sock, so I quickly turned and walked away, certain the dogs and DEA were tailing me. But they weren't, I had lucked out. I didn't consider myself a criminal, but I decided that if I ever did anything "bad" again, I should have a smarter game plan.

The purpose of this compendium is not to turn you into a deviant or a prick. You either have those "qualities" or you don't. Most of the information in this book is perfectly legal, but some of the subjects are not. That doesn't mean there is anything illegal about learning how to do them though. The rogues, the lawbreakers, the cops—they know this stuff, so why shouldn't you? If you choose to remain ignorant under the guise of having a higher standard of morality, that's your call.

In each chapter I have offered up reasons and hypotheticals as to why you might find yourself in need of this manual. Maybe you've been pulled over for going 80 mph in a school zone, but it's because you were too preoccupied composing a text message to realize how fast you were going. Whatever the case may be, inside you'll learn smart ways to get out of that ticket. Let's say you're in college, but, because of the high price of marijuana, you can no longer afford your textbooks. Here, you'll find detailed instructions on how to grow your own. Perhaps you're under a lot of stress and you need to find an additional spouse to abuse. Inside you'll learn how to commit bigamy flawlessly.

So take this journey, and learn how to get an alias or even how to bust out of prison. It's a trip filled with desperation, deception, and, ultimately, redemption.

DERELICT'S SECTION

1. Pass a Polygraph Test

Whether you've been asked to take a lie detector test or need to clear your name, passing a polygraph test is easy—even if you're a sketchy, lying piece of shit. How dare they doubt your veracity? Your taxes helped buy this little toy. You should get to play with the polygraph, too, and question the details of *their* lives. We're all Americans here; didn't Aaron Burr shoot Alexander Hamilton for questioning his honor?

Understand that the test is more akin to black magic than credible science, because it depends on trickery, physiological responses, and the interpretation of an operator—it's just asking to be manipulated by your rogue mind.

Polygraph machines are designed to measure anxiety, so remember that no deceptive strategy will be effective if you fear the polygraph or are plagued by your own guilt. This chapter provides advice about beating the lie detector test, but it will only be useful if you are equipped with a rightful sense of impunity.

Understanding the Machine and the Format of the Test

The polygraph is composed of multiple (poly) sensors that detect your breathing rate, blood pressure, perspiration, and pulse. The interrogation procedure entails a series of relevant and control questions. The latter are intended to make you fib.

An example of a control question is, "Did you ever lie to get out of trouble?" Of course you do not want to answer "yes" to that question while you are taking a lie detector test, but the operator knows that no human can honestly answer "no." The relevant questions are the ones that pertain to the offense for which you have been accused.

The polygraph compares your physiological responses (pulse, breathing rate, blood pressure, perspiration, body movement) to the control questions and your physiological responses to the relevant questions. They are looking for degrees of deviation from "normal," a condition which is established during the preliminary biographical questioning. If you demonstrate more anxiety—a greater deviation from normal—in response to the control questions, then you pass the test; if your anxiety is greater in response to the relevant questions, then you fail the test. If the results are about equal, then the test is deemed inconclusive. In other words, you want your anxiety level to be at its highest when you answer the control questions.

Polygraph manipulation techniques are never foolproof. If you are nervous or concentrate too hard on pulling off a given strategy, then the operator will be alerted to your plan to "beat the machine." The lie detector test is not a battle between man and machine; rather, it is a test of man's control of his own senses. The best advice to give is *relax*. Whether you are telling the truth or not, you need to believe your story and be cognizant of your body. The test may last from one to three hours, and you will be bombarded with questions. If you are not lying, then it will be a breeze—and if you are, stay calm.

Ace the Test

1. Refuse the polygraph if you can, but if you must take it . . .

2. Before you enter the testing facility, acknowledge the absence of science or certainty in the lie-detecting process. The machine will only be effective if you believe in its infallibility, so understand that it is only a machine, not a sorcerer, and answer the questions with confidence and ease.
3. Relax and be wary of the operator's interview tricks. They will try to elicit a confession and take advantage of you if you seem inclined to succumb to intimidation tactics. Remember that the operator does not know anything more than what you have disclosed to him in the preinterview and interview. If your story has credence and consistency, then you will have an advantage.
4. Identify the questions as *control* or *relevant* during the interrogation process, and augment your blood pressure and heart rate when you respond to the control questions. Here are some examples of control question sabotage (perform only one technique at a time):

Control Question Sabotage

- *Develop a breathing strategy.* Throughout the test (except during control questions) maintain a steady breathing rate (example: fifteen to thirty breaths per minute). Do not breathe too deeply. When you are asked a control question, break your breathing pattern by inhaling faster or slower, and make your breathing shallower. Do this for five to fifteen seconds, then resume your normal breathing pattern before you are asked the next question.
- *Stimulate your emotions* by thinking about something exciting, frightening, maddening, or erotic. It is common to try to conceal your emotions, but that takes measurable effort. It is wiser to relax and give

your emotions free range during the interview, intensifying them during the control questions.

- *Bite your tongue* or the side of your mouth. You want to cause pain, but you do not want to draw blood or attract the attention of the operator. Use this strategy during a "yes" or "no" question. This method is not ideal during a verbose answer, because you may not be able to time it correctly. If you plan to employ this method, you must practice at home to perfect the bite strategy.
- *Insert a pin under your toe* and press down on it during the control questions. (This is an older method that is not applicable if the operator asks you to remove your shoes beforehand.)
- If you do not have a pressure-sensitive seat, then you can *contract your sphincter muscle* when a control question is asked. Don't overdo this technique, because if you clench too hard, the graph will spike. Practice this at home first. You want to clench the sphincter and keep the buttocks inert. If you clench your buttocks muscles, then your body will shift.

5. There may be variable questions, such as word association exercises or image tests. During a word association exercise, answer with the first word that comes to mind. If you hesitate or try to search for a less incriminating word, then you actually put yourself at a disadvantage. The polygraph operator tries to eliminate the element of surprise from the test, so if he plans to give you an image test, he will give you some warning. Prepare yourself. Think of something soothing before the image test begins, and stay cool when you actually see the goods.
6. Use every control question technique in moderation. While the machine may not be able to detect every

Figure 1. Rather than trying to conceal your emotions, sabotage your "control" questions by thinking about something exciting, frightening, maddening, or erotic.

countermeasure, there is an operator scrutinizing you for signs of subterfuge.

7. Practice these methods at home to gain mastery before you face the machine.
8. Be consistent! The same questions will be posed numerous times under the guises of different phrasing.

Believe your lies and answer with unequivocal confidence.

Do not fall for the post-interview trickery. The operator will often try to elicit a confession out of you by indicating failing test results, coaxing you into trusting him, or reminding you that there will be a lesser legal penalty if you just confess. Do not give in.

2. Score Prescription Drugs

Oxycontin. Percocet. Vicodin. Prozac. Xanax. Valium. There really is a problem with prescription drugs in the United States, and the biggest problem is that many of us are having a hard time scoring some for ourselves. Why should a basket case or corporate blowhard get the goods, while you, a true drug experimenter are excluded? Moreover, today's power-hungry psychiatrist is putting the honest, hard-working drug dealer out of business.

Sure, if the shrink doesn't think you're sick enough for meds, you can kill him. You may even get away with it by saying it was his fault because he wouldn't give you your medication.

Here are some effective angles.

Methods for Scoring Meds

Be sick. The simplest method of obtaining a prescription is to truly exhibit the symptoms that it treats. You sick, disturbed, lucky bitch.

Friends or family. Purchase the drugs from a friend or family member who has a prescription or can get one. If they won't help you, do you have any friends who are troubled or sickly or both? Might they walk out of a psychiatrist's office with a wallet or purse full of prescriptions? Encourage your loved ones to see a doctor for their own sake. Next, remind them to mention the symptoms that will result in desirable prescriptions. Later offer to buy a few pills off of them. If you are lacking truly sick friends, then turn to your gullible friends. Commandeer their minds. Convince them that they need professional help for a crippling condition and, because you are so concerned, offer to drive them to the doctor yourself.

E-psych. (This option will disappear quickly, so take advantage of it while it's hot.) Visit a psychiatrist on the Web and request the pills. There are online forums in which clients approach psychiatrists with brief descriptions of their ailments and requests for medicine, and the psychiatrists fulfill their needs with prescriptions.

Acting. See a real psychiatrist or doctor about your "maladies." Research the pills that interest you. Which ailments and diseases do they treat? What are the symptoms of those ailments and diseases? Can you fake those symptoms? If so, then see the doctor, put on a show, and take home your shiny new bottle. *Warning:* If you choose to fake a disease, you must be convincing. Do not name the disease or suggest any medication. Pretend that your goal is to figure out what has been plaguing you, and you haven't given *any* thought to medicinal treatment.

Use your kids. Use your teenage child as a psychiatric pawn. Maybe it is time that they see the school psychologist or a private psychologist to discuss their difficulty paying attention in school—you might need to start a campaign of mental abuse to actually make them sick enough to get the meds you want.

Go borderline. Get the pills in Canada or Mexico (there are even Web sites for pill shopping in these more mature North American markets). Or anywhere outside the U.S. and bring them home. There are foreign prescription drug Web sites, but do not shop recklessly online. Be discreet and well informed.

Make sure that Web sites are legit before you give them your information.

Swipe your own pad. Go to an office center that specializes in psychology and sit in the waiting room. Scope out when the doctors leave their offices for the bathroom or lunch breaks. These offices are generally very quiet and don't have any receptionists, office personnel, or nurses. Just those entitled pill gods. Calmly walk into a psychiatrist's office, open the desk

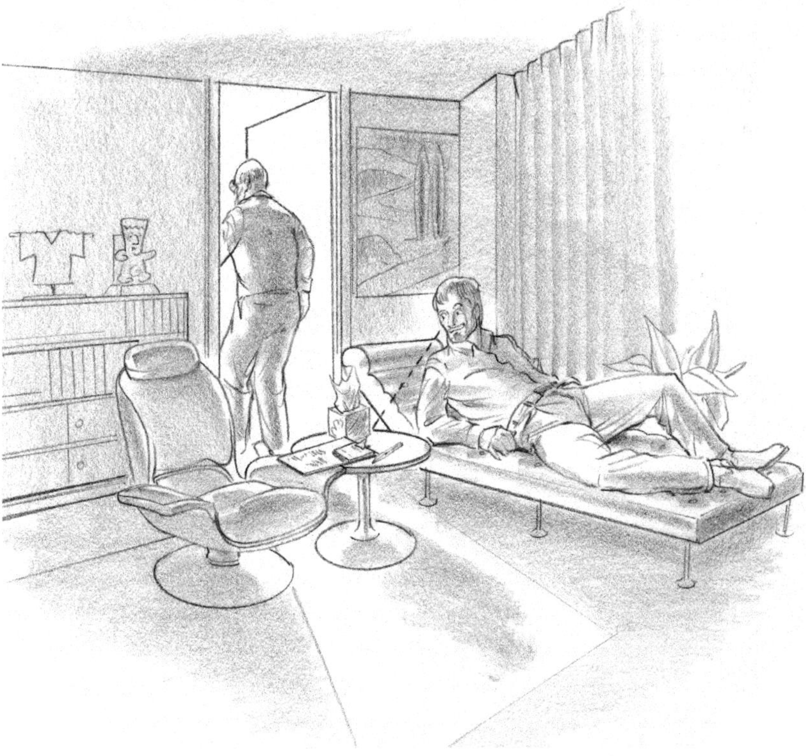

Figure 2. If the opportunity arises, always feel free to tear off a few prescription pages to help you through your difficult time.

drawer, and swipe an unused prescription pad (one that literally has your name on it from now on). Don't feel bad about this; these doctors are practically getting paid off by the pharm companies—*they* are the real thieves.

Overthrow a Pharmacy. This might be a last resort. Scope out a busy drugstore or pharmacy that has places to hide and an evening closing time. Bring a ski mask in your pocket and enter the store at a time when they are busiest and least likely to remember you. Don't do anything that calls attention to yourself. Tuck into your hiding place and wait for the store to close. When everyone has left, put on your ski mask and spring into action—raid the pharmacy and scoop up the meds you want. If you are truly paranoid (hopefully, the meds will cure this, however) or simply extra careful, you can burn down the place to make a statement and destroy any evidence.

LEGENDS OF BAD

Unknown Thieves

Perhaps there is some kind of logic to keeping millions of dollars' worth of pharmaceutical drugs in a nondescript factory warehouse, virtually unguarded. But not to a couple of skilled thieves who stuck it to the Eli Lilly Corp, their overpaid sales force, power-hungry shrinks, and asshole pharmacists everywhere.

During a blustery storm just before daybreak, near Springfield, MA, a team of rogues scaled the brick walls to the top of the building, bore a hole through the roof, turned off the alarms and rapelled down to the floor. They spent hours loading the feel-goods into a moving truck they had parked at the loading dock. Then they simply drove off with the largest pill heist in history, $75 million in wholesale value, including the meds: Zyprexa, Cymbolta and Prozac.

3. Hack a Vending Machine

How many times over the course of your life have you been robbed by a vending machine? Sometimes your food choice gets stuck, and you're just sitting there like a schmuck watching it dangle. How many times have you been confused by the letter or number ordering system? You wanted spicy salsa Doritos and instead you've got yogurt and date trail mix. Maybe it won't accept your soiled dollars and makes it seem like *you* are the filthy one. So, you ask a passer-by if they'll trade bills with you, and they want nothing to do with you, and you don't even blame them.

Sometimes the vending machine flat out steals your money. You want your goddamned money back, so you wait weeks to confront the shylocks who own the vending machines. When they come to collect their cash, they tell you to stay back, like they're safecrackers in the C.I.A.—like you are not on their level. The vending machines have wronged *you*—and now it's time to collect.

Digital Hacking

We live in the gilded age of vending machine hackery. The digital era has introduced some pretty cool computerized vending machines, but the nature of their programming works in favor of hackers. There are ample riches to be found in modern

Coke and Pepsi machines, including gratis colas and buckets of change.

Hackers decode the menus by pressing the machine's buttons in specific numerical patterns. These codes are unique to different vending machines. Rather than write out the decoding patterns for these different machines, it is much simpler for you to go to YouTube and type in "Hack a Vending Machine" in the search bar.

The following old-school hacking techniques are not specific to any particular model and hard drive. Just good old fashioned theft.

The "Taped" Bill Method

1. *Use clear packing tape* to tape both sides of a dollar bill.
2. *Leave one inch of the bill exposed* (on both sides), and insert that end first.
3. Make sure there are *no air bubbles.*
4. *Create a tail of tape* (about four or five feet long), and hold the end of the tail while the bill is fed into the machine.
5. After you have made your selection, and it registers, carefully *pull the bill back out* of the machine.

Other Methods

Saltwater it. Pour a saltwater mixture into a coin slot (you may have to sip the mixture in your mouth and spit it in there, and possibly chase it with a single coin to ensure proper flow of the liquid). This will short-circuit the machine, and it typically results in a free soda or two. If sodas are not immediately dispensed, just press a selection button and be prepared for the machine to spew soda bottles and buck. It may also emit change.

Smash it. If there are no cameras around (and newer machines have interior cameras), then smash the glass with a table leg, hammer, or some heavy instrument. Take the loot and run. Also, you can try tilting the machine.

Figure 3. Leave the first inch of the bill exposed and attach a "tail" of packing tape. Insert the bill, and once it registers, pull it back out by the tail.

The abortion. If the machine has a clear window, straighten out a wire hanger, lift the flap where the snacks drop, and snake the wire up into the machine. Poke a hole in the wrapper or just spear the food that has caught your eye.

Slugs or fake coins. Affix a fake or real coin on a string, and reuse it on any vending machine.

4. Get Out of the Armed Forces

Some people join the armed forces to gain discipline, some join out of a duty to their country, and others join because they've been conned by a high-school recruiter. However, if getting harassed by an over-the-top drill sergeant just isn't for you, and you have realized that you made a mistake there are ways to get out.

Honorable Discharge

If you are in the first days of service and you are still enrolled in a training program, then you may be eligible for an Entry-Level Separation. You must begin the paperwork for this separation within the first 180 days, so act quickly. Your commanding officer must determine that your continued presence in the military would be detrimental to the collective unit, so start convincing. Have hysterical outbursts, refuse to eat, weep, throw tantrums, become a zealous, conscientious objector, threaten people in absurd ways (promise someone that you will turn him into a lizard and then keep him as your lover), ride an invisible motorcycle everywhere you go, speak gibberish, disobey commands, and so on.

Conscientious Objector

A conscientious objector (CO) is one who opposes war on all grounds. Their beliefs need to challenge the premise that war is an effective means to resolve national or international disputes. Be all the CO you can be in the Army. Be theatrical (but believable). Refuse to engage in any practice activities, refuse to follow any orders issued by a superior, make philosophical speeches on the futility of warfare, stage hunger strikes, distribute anti-war propaganda, enlist other members of your unit to join the cause, do anything you can to subvert the daily operations of your commanding officer's unit. If the commanding officer does not approach you to address the problem, then approach him. Typically, COs are required to speak with a counselor who will determine whether or not they are fit for service. Try to be subtle enough to convince the counselor that you will not be an asset to your unit. Explain why you are a conscientious objector in the most lucid manner possible. Rehearse a speech if you must. You should include personal philosophy and personal experience in your statement. If you want to claim that you now subscribe to a pacifist religious doctrine, then so be it. Persuade the counselor that you are not the same person who enlisted, and you cannot carry out the orders of a military entity that operates on principles that defy your personal belief system.

Behavioral Disorder

If you don't think you can work the cognitive angle, then take an antithetical approach: Go crazy. Gradually sink into insanity—don't do it overnight. Start zoning out, then graduate to naked strolls into the mess hall, and eventually, smear the gruel into the design of a dress on your naked body. Tell people to look out for the killer unicorn that has been storming your barracks for the past few nights. Violently attack yourself (don't hurt anyone else, but instill a healthy fear in them). When your commanding officer approaches you, tell him that you feel fine. You will ultimately be sent to a behavior analyst,

Figure 4. One inventive soldier actually rode around his base on an imaginary cycle. He was soon released from duty.

and as long as your insanity does not seem like a performance, you will most likely be asked to leave.

Homosexuality

Make passes at your commanding officer and other members of your unit. The issue will be addressed immediately, and you can sign a form that affirms your homosexuality. This will likely lead to a discharge.

AWOL

Of course, you could desert and risk the consequences of capture. (A warrant will be issued for your arrest, but it is likely that you will not be apprehended.)

5. Make a Molotov Cocktail

With an accurate throw that lands in the fuel tank, you can blow up an army tank. But even if you're not rioting, it's always good to know how to make this improvised incendiary device. It's a good way to make a memorable first impression at your new church. During the sermon, use your bomb to blow apart the front door. When the fire begins to wane, casually enter the church and claim to be Satan.

Yet just as technology continues to evolve, so does the Molotov cocktail. The classic model consists of using an oil-soaked rag as the wick. But this method can backfire, as the fuel can easily escape from the bottle, or worse, the explosive can blow up in your hand. The modern Molotov actually employs a tampon to maximize effectiveness.

Step-by-Step Instructions

The bottle

1. Start with a glass container such as a wine bottle or liquor canister. Whatever vessel you use, make sure that you still have the cork or cap.

The mixture. There are a couple of options for use as your flammable fluid, depending on the desired effect.

2. Fill your bottle with *50 percent gasoline / 50 percent motor oil.* Motor oil ignites easily and it will stick to your target.

   Or use 50 percent gasoline / 50 percent tar. Tar burns hotter than motor oil and is also very sticky.
3. Place lid on bottle.
4. Shake well.

The tampon wick. Rather than using an oily rag, a gas-soaked tampon is much more effective.

5. Soak a tampon with gas.
6. Fasten the tampon to the neck or side of the bottle with two rubber bands.

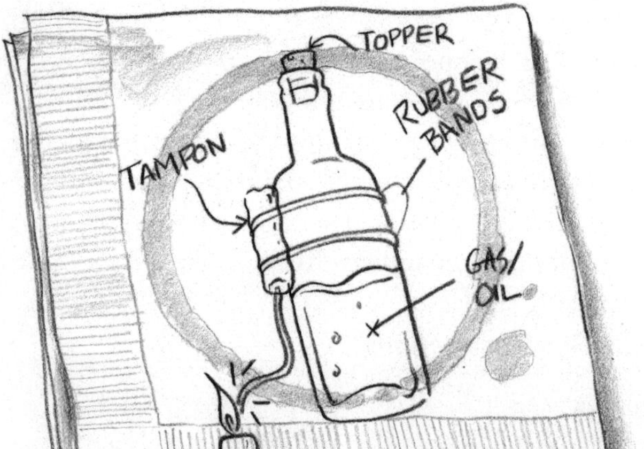

Figure 5. There are few things sexier than using a gas-soaked tampon to blow something up.

The bomb

7. Light the string of the tampon as your fuse.
8. Throw the bottle hard at your target. It must break in order for it to ignite.
9. Enjoy the explosion.

6. Create an Alias

There are many reasons you might want or need an alias—and none of them are any of our business. Maybe being bound to your birth name is keeping you from truly expressing your views. Why not create an alias alter ego to take the heat for your legal transgressions? When you're working at your bank job, you're Mike Smith, but on your internet blog dedicated to toppling the capitalist system, you're Jake Jenson. Mike Smith pays the mortgage and votes for local officials, but Jake Jenson is in the process of establishing an autonomous nation in a camper on Mike Smith's property. When cashiers at department stores ask Mike Smith for his name and zip code, they receive Jake Jenson's information, because you never know who is cooperating with a secret F.B.I. investigation.

The great news is that owning an assumed name in America is quite simple and legal. In fact, one's right to create a new name is guaranteed under the Fourteenth Amendment of the U.S. Constitution.

The "Usage" Method

Or say you have an exhausting name, such as Michael Saltalamacchia, and would like to become Jake Jenson. It's easy. Just pick your assumed name and start using it. Done.

Most U.S. states allow you to change your name for any reason, with no paperwork or legal proceedings. The government won't have any issue unless they can prove you changed your name for fraudulent intent such as avoiding bankruptcy. They also don't approve of names with symbols or numbers, or any words of an obscene nature. The *usage method* is also referred to as *at will* or *common law.*

Follow these steps:

1. *Choose your alias carefully.* You can alter your first name, middle name, last name, or all three. Practice your autograph. Ask a couple of people you know to start calling you by it. See how it sounds.
2. Once you've chosen your alias, you must use it consistently with all relevant parties. It's your alias, so enjoy it. If you plan to use your alias with those who already know you by your given name (friends, family, coworkers, agencies, and any businesses with which you have contact), you must notify them and use the alias exclusively. If people doubt you, *let them know you are serious,* and that you have legally changed your name. Soon it will stick.
3. In most states, the usage method is considered a *legal* way to change your name. As such, you may *obtain a driver's license with your alias* and use that to get a social security card, credit cards, and even a passport.

"Court Petition" Method

In some states, certain institutions, such as banks and government agencies, may require a court order to officially ratify your alias.

To get your court-approved alias, you should contact your appropriate local government office and ask the clerk for a *petition for name change* and any other related paperwork. This process generally requires that you pay a small fee, and that you publish a legal notice in your local newspaper in case

Figure 6. Go to Mexico and get brand-new documentation. While you're there, pick up some illegal firecrackers and cheap whores.

there are any objectors. After that, a judge has legal discretion to grant or deny your alias. Usually, the only way the judge will not allow the name change is if there is a legitimate objection, or if he or she believes your alias is for fraudulent use. Plus, if you can't afford it, there's even a fee waiver option. Just ask the clerk.

Or, to make things even easier, you can hire legal services, even online, that will help you secure your alias. Though, if you are creating an alias, you may not want to spill such information into legal cyberspace.

LEGENDS OF BAD

Christian Karl Gerhartsreiter

A.k.a. Chris Chichester, a.k.a. Christopher C. Crowe, a.k.a. Michael Brown, a.k.a. Clark Rockefeller, a.k.a. J. P. Clark Rockefeller, a.k.a. Clark M. Rockefeller III, a.k.a. Clark Mills Rockefeller, a.k.a. James Frederick, a.k.a. Charles Smith, a.k.a. Chip Smith.

Gerhartsreiter truly lived the American dream. He came to the United States as a German foreign exchange student and quickly made a name for himself—Chris Chichester. Soon after, Chichester begat Christopher Crowe, who for years was sought as a suspect in the murder of a missing man. Along the way, Gerhartsreiter picked up an additional slew of aliases until he landed on his favorite, Clark Rockefeller. It was a brilliant choice, as he claimed to be an heir to the billion dollar Rockefeller family. Clark Rockefeller began circulating in high society circles, even joining the elite Algonquin Club where he served as a board member. Rockefeller married a wealthy, hard-working woman who bore him a daughter and supported him, as he chose not to work. He did this to network, so he could spread his good name. The wife divorced him, however, and got custody, leaving him no choice but to kidnap his daughter. A few months later, he was arrested as Charles "Chip" Smith.

Underage Alias

Minors can create a legal alias, too. Here's how:

1. Obviously, the usage method is easiest. Simply *start using your new alias in your daily life.* With your new alias, high school will never be the same. Just tell your peers, teachers, and the school administration that you've changed your name.
2. If your state makes you go the official route, *a consent form from your legal guardian is required.*
3. However, if you're having difficulty obtaining consent, you may go to your local courthouse or government institution to *file a petition of name change.* Then, ask the clerk for a formal delivery notice, served to your guardian. This news is delivered either via sheriff *or* certified mail.

Create a DBA (Doing Business As)

A DBA is the legal use of a business alias. A DBA allows you to promote, make transactions, and represent yourself under an assumed name. Obtaining a DBA is relatively easy and costs little. Filing procedures differ from state to state, so check with your local government clerk's office and ask for the appropriate paperwork. They'll ask you to search a database to ensure your alias isn't already taken.

The "El Seudnimo" Method

A more nefarious, and illegal, option is to cross the Mexican border and pick up bogus documentation, then reenter the U.S. under your alias. Whatever your budget, the papers you need are just around the corner. Generally, within minutes, you'll be approached and offered U.S. residency cards, Social Security cards, and if you pay enough, you can easily score a phony—yet flawless—American passport. You can also obtain an actual "green card"—with a photo of someone resembling your likeness. (In this case, the more Latino you are, the better.) These shadier options also exist here in America. Phony documentation is sold openly in places such as East Los Angeles or Tucson. If you want it bad enough, corrupt officials at the D.M.V. can always be found.

7. Pick a Lock

When you know how to pick a lock, so many doors open up to you. Shopping at boutiques is that much easier when you don't have to kowtow to store hours, sales people, or prices. And even though the hot new girl in your apartment complex turned you down for a date, you can get a second chance to make a memorable impression by entering her bedroom, unannounced. Of course, if people were as friendly as you are, you wouldn't have to break into their homes because their doors would already be unlocked.

Yale Lock

The urban legend is true—you can open a Yale lock with a plastic card. (Don't use a credit card, because you may wear down the card in the process.) Rub the narrow side of the card against the latch while jiggling the lock. After a few minutes of work, the lock should give.

Deadbolt

This is the most difficult lock to break. Deadbolts vary by length of throw, which is the depth of the bolt's penetration of the door jamb.

- You may be able to *saw through a deadbolt,* but beware of steel shanks in the center.

- You may also *use a drill (in a remote area) to remove the lock or tamper with the knob, or use a tool to pry the deadbolt out of its track.*
- *Use a pick and tension wrench, or torque wrench, to pick the lock.* (You may also use a pick gun, which pushes up all of the pins at once.) You will need a flathead screwdriver, as well.
    1. *Insert the torque wrench in the lower portion of the keyhole* and turn the cylinder as far as it will go (toward the right).
    2. *Insert the pick* in the upper portion of the keyhole, and feel around for the pins in the lock (these pins are manipulated by the key, so you should insert the pick as you would a key; patiently feel around to find the pins that you must push up).

Figure 7. Defeat the deadbolt with a lock pick and tension wrench.

3. *Turn your tension wrench* as you push the pins up, and keep repeating this method until you have pushed each pin up and set the lock.
4. *Turn the torque wrench* one last time, and use a flat-head screwdriver to unlock it.

Padlock

By using a cut-out piece of aluminum as a "shim," one can get inside of the ball-locking mechanism on a master padlock and unlock it. Rather than illustrate the process here, you can watch it demonstrated on YouTube under "Open a padlock with a beer can."

Chain Lock

Kick it in or saw it.

8. Get Out of Jury Duty

Though having the fate of some poor sap in your hands sounds pretty cool, and having the power to continually exasperate a tired room of jurors can be an awesome experience, there are, in fact, good reasons to get out of jury duty. Here are more legitimate ones, as well as more creative techniques.

Escapes *Before* Serving

- ***Financial Grounds.*** If you are in a state that excuses jurors on financial grounds, then you can bring financial statements and tax forms to the courthouse to prove that you cannot afford to miss work. Do not use phony tax forms—if you make too much money for this trick, then use a different evasion method.
- ***Already a Volunteer.*** If you are already a volunteer for a reputable organization, then you are already doing your civic duty. Get a letter from your captain, chief, or guru excusing you from jury duty.
- ***You're a Caretaker.*** If you care for children or elderly people who depend on your presence, you may be able to get a postponement or a dismissal.
- ***You're Irreplaceable.*** If your presence is critical to the operation of a business, you may be able to get a postponement or a dismissal.

- ***Ironclad Excuse.*** Think of an ironclad excuse and request a change of date when you receive your jury notification. Joining the military, suffering from a terminal illness, battling a psychological disorder, traveling for work, or moving to care for a sick relative will most likely set the date back one year.
- ***Change the Date.*** Ask to change your serve-date to an earlier day. Your name will be appended to a list that has already been composed, and most likely you will not even be summoned. Failing this, you could ask to move your date to December, which means that there is more of a chance that the trial will be rescheduled.
- ***Call the Judge.*** Make phone calls to ask the judge and clerk for waivers.

Escapes *While* Serving

- Begin to *ask questions about "jury nullification,"* which gives a jury the power to declare a defendant not guilty on the grounds that the law is unjust and, therefore, nullified (in the context of this case). Boldly ask the attorneys and the judge as many questions as you can about this legal phenomenon. This will depict you as a dissident, or at least a potential irritant, and you may be dismissed.
- Be too eager to *support the prosecution's case* without hearing the full defense. Adopt a stubborn persona, and refuse to change your mind in issues regarding the trial. Play stubborn and ignorant.
- Conversely, if you *appear too well-informed* on the subject, you may also be dismissed. If this particular crime strikes a personal note with you (because a friend or relative was involved in a case like this in the past), then speak up. If you happen to know any of the witnesses or

Figure 8. To get out of serving, sometimes your best defense is to get offensive.

cops, or you are familiar with the area in which the crime was committed, be vocal about it. If you happen to be a specialist in any aspect of this case, then don't hesitate to inject your expertise into the conversation despite the fact that the lawyers and judges want you to hush.

- *Convince the judge, lawyers, and your fellow jurors* that you are neither objective nor stable during the introductory process. You can accomplish this through theatrical responses to details of the case (gasp, clutch your face, squawk the occasional outburst). Maintaining a general moronic demeanor (pretend not to understand simple concepts) won't hurt. You must be subtle and sincere in this performance. Don't overdo it, because these officials see people try to get out of jury duty every day.

- Look or smell unappealing. Go into the courthouse wearing pajamas, or avoid taking a shower for a few days before your jury duty begins. You may just be reprimanded and ordered to clean yourself up, but there is a good chance that they will give you a waiver to reduce their headache potential.

9. Shoplift

Most shoplifters are law abiding citizens who have never been arrested. They don't use shoplifting paraphernalia, they don't do drugs, they have proper ID, yet, even so, they are compelled to shoplift. According to experts, that's because the adrenaline rush of getting something for nothing is the same as the chemical addiction people get from extreme sports. That must mean stealing a bungee cord it the ultimate high.

Shoplifting must be done with self-control. Impulsive thieves are always caught because their pockets are bulging with merchandise (and anti-theft sensors) when they leave the store. Survey the surveillance. If there are too many cameras, then you are not destined to steal tonight. You can only swipe goods from aisles with little foot traffic and no security.

Fitting Rooms

Get to know store policies in the fitting rooms. Are there employees monitoring the fitting rooms or do people let themselves in and out without assistance? If the fitting rooms are private, then bring your shopping bags (that you brought from home or stole from another store) into the room with you. Gracefully drop an item or two into them. Make sure that those items have no sensors. Do not do this too quickly, and do not spend too much time in the fitting room, either. Take only one or two garments, and put the rest of the clothes back on the racks.

The misdirection. Identify the item that you want to steal from the shelves, and begin examining a completely different piece of merchandise. While you are playing with the distraction piece, you are sliding the desired item into your bag with your free hand or your foot.

Figure 9. Insert one or two articles of clothing into a labeled shopping bag from another store, make sure no sensors are attached, then walk out casually.

Pocket it. If you cannot spot security or spectators, simply swipe the goods and calmly walk out of the store.

Tag swap. Change the way you think about shoplifting. Instead of planning to take materials for nothing, make a plan to pay less than what they are worth. Simply peel the tags off one item and adhere it to another. You can do this a number of times with different items, but make sure that you have a full basket of items when you approach the cashier.

10. Evade Surveillance

We are constantly being tracked—the cameras are everywhere—at work, on the bus, shopping, walking the dog (See Chapter 16: Avoid Cleaning Up After Your Dog). Our computers, our cell phones, and our credit cards inform numerous government agencies and private companies about exactly where we are and what we are saying. How are you supposed to chat on your favorite cannibalism Web site when freaks like "Tom" from Myspace are this far up your ass? Even if you simply have a case of crippling paranoia, it will actually strengthen your ability to succeed.

You Know You're Being Followed When . . .

If you are involved in any illicit activities, you should just assume that you are being watched. That will give you an edge. If you are embroiled in a divorce case, you have just filed an insurance claim for an injury, or you are cheating on a suspicious spouse, then there is a good chance that you will be tailed.

- *You will notice* an unfamiliar car in the neighborhood, you will notice someone following you in public, and/or, from a distance, you will notice someone taking pictures of you, your property, or your surroundings.
- *Friends may report* that they have received phone calls inquiring about you, or you may experience more hang-ups and wrong numbers.

- Your car or briefcase may be wired with a tracking device, or your phone may be bugged (you will have to actually *inspect all of your belongings* and dismantle the electronics to find some of these devices).
- *Your house may be monitored* by a voice or a video recorder that has been covertly placed in a wall, in a wall fixture, or in an appliance.

Evasion Techniques

There are numerous ways to handle an investigator, some of which involve avoidance, and one of which involves confrontation:

- *Confront the suspected snoop and ask him what he is trying to uncover.* He won't admit that he is investigating you, but at least you will make him uneasy and make his job much more difficult.
- *Once you have confronted the investigator, begin following him.* Follow him until he leaves you alone. You can follow him while he intends to follow you, but you can also take it a step further and follow him home to his own neighborhood.

The evasive tactics are more complicated:

- *Identify alternate exits to your house* (basement door, hidden windows, storm door, vent, and so on), and use them all regularly, without relying on any particular pattern of circulation.
- *Speak in code on the phone and in your house*—never disclose the location of any nefarious activities or the names of any of your colleagues.
- Either *keep an erratic schedule to throw off the investigator,* or keep such a mundane schedule that you will deceive him with the lull of routine.

Figure 10. Secret exits and entrances will make surveillance more difficult. Or confront the investigator, begin to follow him, and put the intrusive bastard on the defensive.

- Even if you don't have a job, *set aside "working hours" during which you do secretive deeds.* Whenever you are going to commit an illegal act, arrive at a consistent location that he will consider "the office," and lose him after you walk in the door. While he tries to crack the mystery of this job, you slip out the back (but keep your car in the lot), and conduct the real business that you don't want him to see. (Note: If you spend all day at a real job that he knows about, then invent this as a second job or just a once-a-month responsibility—perfect if you are concealing an affair.)

Hack Surveillance Cameras on Google

In a matter of seconds, you can go from looking at a lame spreadsheet at work to looking at hundreds of unsuspecting people through a parade of surveillance cameras. Go to Householdhacker.com where you can access a list of Web addresses to be cut and pasted into your address bar. Almost immediately, you are streamlined into a network of live security cameras from around the country. It's not even illegal. Sure, it may be creepy, but at least you're not the one being watched.

11. Beat a Speeding Ticket

It's a typical day on the road. You're going 80 mph in a school zone, and texting your coke dealer. Out of nowhere, flashing blue and red lights flood your rearview mirror. They make you pull over. They scold you like a child. Why should you take this?

Between the moment that you are pulled over and the moment that you are found guilty—and fined for your speeding offense—you are provided two escape passages. You will find the keys to those portals in either the ticketing officer's compassion or the judge's legal code.

Escape Opportunity #1: Charm the Police

- As you safely pull over, you need to *compose yourself and prepare to be as respectful as possible* to the police officer. (If you are definitely being pulled over for a speeding violation, take note of the closest speed limit sign.)
- *Turn off your car, and quickly find your license, registration, and insurance information.* Then place your hands at 10 and 2 on your steering wheel to await the cop's approach. (Never step out of the car, and do not reach into your pockets to retrieve anything without notifying the officer beforehand.) The key is to be submissive and acknowledge the officer's authority. You do not want to move around or seem cagey while you are in the car, be-

cause your movement will put him on edge and undercut his feeling of control. If the officer feels in control of the situation from the onset, then he will be more inclined to be lenient once you begin speaking.

- If the officer does not immediately engage in a discussion about the violation, then *let him conduct his business silently* (punctuated by an occasional sheepish, "I'm sorry" from you). Often, the police officer is gauging your jerk factor in the first few minutes of the encounter, so not saying anything is the best way to ensure that you don't say anything wrong.
- Once the officer has obtained your information, *request to speak to him about your violation.* Remember to ask rather than demand. When he explains the citation, do not argue with his judgment. Concede his points and sincerely apologize for your recklessness. Plead your case in a succinct, repentant manner. This is the crucial moment in which the officer determines whether or not you really deserve the ticket. If you pull off the remorseful, obedient citizen routine, you are not clear yet, because the variable is the cop's degree of mercy. A slight tear trickle may help a woman's case here (effeminate men, perhaps, too). A woman can also say that she's having her period so she can quickly get to a bathroom. At the end of your conversation, the officer will deliver his verdict.

Escape Opportunity #2: Beat the Police

- If the cop proceeds to write you a ticket, *ask him about his radar.* Many, but not all, jurisdictions require that cops disclose that information upon request. If he refuses, respect his refusal and wait to pursue it during your court appearance.

Figure 11. Evaluate your attitude. Your facial expression should be apologetic and your speech should be minimal. No pleas, no excuses, no indignant outbursts, no speaking (until spoken to), and your hands should be in the 10 and 2 o'clock position.

- *You might ask,* "When was the last time your radar gun was calibrated?" or "Where were you when you clocked my speed?" or "Were you moving when you clocked my speed?"
- *Ask about the radar unit's certification.* Many radar technicians provide a certificate of accuracy to the officer after the unit is placed in service.
- *Ask if the officer has been trained in the specific use of the radar unit* inside the vehicle he was driving at the time of the stop. Many times agencies exchange old equipment for new, which allows a period of time before the officer can train on the new equipment. Do not use an argumentative tone when you inquire about the radar

gun; simply express your curiosity and tell him that you want to be informed for your court appearance.

- *Take your ticket and politely drive away without leaving an impression on the officer.* Police officers remember those who irk them, but acquiescent citizens fade into memory vapor.
- Before you go to court, you can *contact the ticketing officer via phone or mail and request that he reevaluate his decision.* You need to use tact and persuasion here. Remember to acknowledge his power and your legal transgression before you even make your case. When you make your case, you must provide a story, rather than just a phobia of tickets. Explaining that you work full-time and cannot afford to take a day off to appear in court will be more effective than sobbing about your driving record.
- You may *plead your case to the presiding judge* and/or prosecutor before your trial date by the same means. If they do not respond, then do not pursue communication with them. Wait for your day in court.

Escape Opportunity #3: Beat the Court

Treat all court employees with deference and respect. Be friendly over the phone and be sure to arrive at your court date early. Never miss any deadlines, make friendly conversation with the court clerk, and develop an affable, yet understated, persona, as well.

- Your ticket is an affidavit in which a police officer attests to your violation of a traffic law. *Read the citation thoroughly.* The wrong streets, dates, or times can be cause for dismissal. Court dates given on holidays may also cause the citation to be dismissed.
- You may be able to *negotiate alternative punishment,* like traffic school. This would keep the ticket off your record and prevent a spike in your insurance premium.

- *Use legal loopholes.* If you delay the trial date by asking for continuances, then you will fade farther and farther from the forefront of the officer's memory. He may even retire or transfer before the final court date, which constitutes a dismissal.
- If you were caught speeding in an area where the *speed limit changes* within a few yards, this can be cause for dismissal in some jurisdictions.
- When you initially appear in court, *have a strategy.* Scope out the court ahead of time so that you know what to wear (not too casual, not too formal), where to sit, and how to conduct yourself properly. During the trial, plead "not guilty," and you will be assigned a court date.
- Matlock the trial. When you arrive at the courthouse, you should *be confident and stoic.* You may attempt to speak to the officer or prosecutor before the trial to cut a deal, but do not be aggressive. There is always the possibility that the officer won't show up, which is grounds for dismissal.

There is a basic trial procedure: The prosecution makes their case against you, you defend yourself (with witnesses if you want to be theatrical), the prosecution rebuts your argument, and the judge makes a decision.

12. Become a Porn Producer

Watching porn is pretty cool—especially if it's unfolding live in your own living room or in the "fuck bus" that you've rented. Not only have technological advances made movie-making simpler and more affordable than ever, but the influx of females with insecurity issues—whether it's from the media's objectification of women, absentee fathers, or abusive boyfriends—have truly made this a golden era in sex. Promiscuous girls just want to know that someone thinks they are pretty or smart enough, and they often get this affirmation from sexual intimacy. Spreading images of these women having sex on the Internet, or showing them to your friends, at the very least, helps women get the reassurance they need. Good job.

Getting Started

Before immersing yourself in the industry, you should research your legal parameters.

- *Know the zoning laws in your area and the local penalties* imposed on those who commit "unnatural acts" or who break laws against obscenity. These laws vary by district.
- *Obtain legal ID from everyone affiliated with your new endeavor* to ensure that your staff is well above the legal age (which also varies—it is twenty-one in some states and eighteen in others).

If you want to become a producer, you should start with the basics:

Tools

1. A quality *digital camcorder.*
2. High-quality *blank tapes.*
3. Video *editing software* (and knowledge).
4. Plenty of *lighting*—you can never have too much lighting. Halogen floor and work lamps are inexpensive, and they provide intense light. When your films pull in more money, you may want to invest in higher quality video-lighting equipment.

Figure 12. Besides lots of good, clean, balls-out sex, having sufficient lighting is integral to filming quality porn. Halogen floor and work lamps are a smart yet inexpensive option.

Space. Once you are well versed on your local zoning laws, you may decide on a shooting space. Home settings are ideal because they are cheap, safe, and low-key. You may film in your home or the home of a friend who is willing to turn over his living space in exchange for the glory of participating in a porn (just make sure that you have a clear understanding of his zoning laws before you begin). Hotels are a preferable alternative, but you need to choose the right hotel, since you are essentially filming illegal porn on their premises. Someplace too seedy may give you less privacy and less lighting, so an expensive, insular room (penthouse style) would provide the best setting. You will probably need to add your own lighting, so you need to plan a discrete method of lighting transport from the hotel lobby to your room.

Actors. There are myriad ways to recruit optimum porn talent:

- There are *adult modeling Web sites* that will allow you to post ads for actors.
- *There are plenty of horny young people* looking to make a few bucks after hours in late night diners, twenty-four-hour department stores, nightclubs, and so on.
- *Place an ad* in a local alternative paper or sex-oriented magazine.
- *Ask somebody* you know.
- Start a local phenomenon that will *capture the interest of aspiring porn stars* in the area. A traveling porn circus will not need to dedicate too much time to star searching, because the stars will flock to it. This method also promotes itself to potential customers.

Filming

The actors will look to you for guidance, so you need to have a plan in mind. Your first porn should mimic the qualities that you seek when you watch these videos. You need to provide clear directions for your actors during the shoot, and it may feel a bit awkward at first. It will take a while to acclimate to this new role, but once you establish a style, it will become much easier.

Editing

The quality of the editing software must be matched by the quality of your editing knowledge. Edit out the scenes that you consider obscene. As you establish your style, your imagery should remain consistent. Your customers will gravitate to your films because they share your taste, so when you see something that turns you off in the video, there is a good chance that it will disturb your viewers, as well. Make sure that the edits don't impede the flow. Choppy porn tends to be anti-climatic.

Promotion and Distribution

There are Web sites that specialize in pornography distribution, so you may contact a Web site and pitch your video to them. If you promote the video yourself, then you need to create a buzz through sensationalism (nothing illegal—just unique).

13. Count Cards in Blackjack

Feeling remorse for counting cards in blackjack is like fighting for your stolen lunch money back and then apologizing to the bully. In fact, if you feel anything other than outright jubilation by outsmarting a slimy casino or a trusted friend, then you deserve to piss away your cash like the fool you are. If winning free money from unscrupulous, oxygen-pumping casinos isn't pay enough, it also sometimes helps you get laid—whether it's the chain-smoking skank you are helping to win beside you, or having the cash to buy that 3-way at the Chicken Ranch.

Card counting is a blackjack strategy used to determine when a player has a probability advantage over the dealer. Even when playing blackjack using perfect basic strategy, the house advantage is still .5 percent. But by counting cards a player can achieve a 1.0 percent advantage over the house. It is in no way illegal, though many casino establishments have a right to eject you if they believe you are doing it. It's actually quite simple, and contrary to popular myth, one does not need to be a mathematical wizard or *Rain Man*-esque to figure it out.

The logic behind counting cards is to bet more money when there are a higher amount of tens, face cards, and aces remaining in a single deck or a multi-deck shoe and to bet less money when there are a higher amount of small cards in the deck. When a player is counting cards, he or she tracks the cards that are being dealt and keeps a running *plus* or *minus* count.

The KO Method

1. *Understand basic blackjack strategy.* If you don't already know it, you can print out a wallet-size chart online to bring to the table.
2. *Wait for the dealer to begin a new deck* or shoe before you begin to play.
3. Place your initial bet and *start your running "count" at zero.*
4. *Subtract* one (-1) point for every 10, jack, queen, king, and ace that is dealt to the table.
5. *Add* one (+1) for every 2, 3, 4, 5, 6, or 7 that is dealt to the table.
6. *Assign* zero points for every 8 or 9 that is dealt to the table.
7. When there is a "positive count," which means there is a higher ratio of tens, faces, and aces than normal, you should *place a higher bet.*

Why You Win

When you are in a positive count, you have a much better chance of winning.

- The dealer will bust more often. Not only do *lower cards hurt your chances at getting quality hands,* smaller cards help the dealer *make* their soft hands.
- *The player will be dealt more blackjacks,* which pay 1.5 to 1.
- *The player will be dealt stronger and higher starting hands.*
- *The player will have a better chance of winning "insurance" bets.*

More advanced card counting systems include Hi-Lo, Hi-Opt 1, Hi-Opt II, Zen Count, and Omega II.

Figure 13. Once you've mastered your card-counting technique, use your winnings to order that 3-way from your bucket list. The Chicken Ranch Bordello: 10511 Homestead Road, Pahrump, NV.

LEGENDS OF BAD

Ken Uster

Ken Uster legally won over $12 million from casinos using his brilliant team-card-counting technique. Then the casinos banned him. But Uster wasn't deterred, and disguised himself, once as a truck driver, winning an enormous hand. But when he was caught in disguise and halted yet again, Uster changed his tack and, in turn, bent over the casinos in an entirely new way: he sued them for banning "skilled players" from tables, won the decision, and was again allowed to take their money.

14. Cheat at Poker

If you are one of these guys who plays poker and punches a wall after losing a pot with two dollars in it, then you definitely need to employ a few of the tactics outlined below. Good poker is about reading your opponents' hands and having guts. So, if you have the guts to literally look at opponents' hands, then this chapter is for you.

Shorting

Sometimes mistakes happen, and you end up putting less than your fair share into the pot. If somebody can prove that you shorted the pot, simply explain that it was an honest mistake.

Peeking

It's easy to get cramped up while sitting at a table all night. Crane your neck, as if you're stretching, to get a good view of a neighboring hand or drop a chip to the floor and sneak a peek. It's also a good idea to get a glance at the bottom card of the deck, as the dealer spits out the hand. If anybody challenges you, look them directly in the eye, and call them a liar.

The Pot Helper

You've folded your hand, yet who says you still can't come out a winner. Being the great guy that you are, appoint yourself the tender of the pot. As the play continues, count out the pot, stack the chips, but before you push the pot to the winning player, be sure to palm a few chips for yourself. There are odorless adhesives that help with this method.

Hand-Mucking

Sometimes you don't like the hand you've been dealt. That's why you can switch your lousy hand with one you've secretly hidden.

Sleight of Hand

Everyone loves magicians, and, if you practice long enough, you make other people's money disappear! A skilled cardsman can learn to *cull* the cards they need by dealing oneself or a confidant the second card from the top, the bottom card, or even the second bottom card off the bottom of the deck. In order to have maximum control of the deck, you will probably have to employ the "mechanic's grip," wherein you'll grip the deck with your index finger in front of it. (Note: If you spot somebody else using the mechanic's grip, be sure to call them out on it—because you *will not* stand for cheaters!)

The Double Duke

You may arrange yourself a wonderful hand, but if there's nobody else on the table with a decent hand your winnings will be minimal. The *double duke* is when the dealer arranges a formidable hand for another player that keeps them in the pot, but, ultimately, loses to your superior hand.

The Cold Deck

Some advantage-takers are able to sleekly introduce a deck that has already been preordered to their liking. Use your

Figure 14. If the back of the deck features a circular design, use it as a face of a clock, and mark the cards' numerical value accordingly.

sleight of hand skills and make a phony cut to ensure all is up and up.

Card Marking

Winning at poker is so much easier if you can tell a card's value from a marking on the back of the card. There are numerous ways to mark cards, here are few common techniques:

- *The Clock.* If the back of the cards have a round figure in the design you can mark the cards using that figure as a clock. For example, you would make a small mark at the one o'clock area of the round figure to mark an ace, a mark at two o'clock for a two, all the way up to twelve o'clock for a queen. A king would have no mark.
- *Shading.* You can premark certain cards in the sun, perhaps royals, to slightly alter the coloring on the back.

- ***Daub*** is a substance one can subtly apply to the back of cards during play, and once mastered, can be read easily from across a table.

Poker Collusion

This is when two players are working in concert to achieve their poker goals. Common forms of collusion include:

- ***Signaling.*** When two players collude by sending each other messages during the game. One method is to stack chips in a certain way to indicate a player's hand or cards.
- ***Soft Playing.*** This is when a player will not raise against his partner during a pot in order to help him save money.
- ***Whipsawing.*** When collaborators keep raising each other in an effort to drive up the pot by trapping unsuspecting players in between them.
- ***Dumping.*** When a player folds in order to let his partner get the pot.

Online Poker

One cannot manipulate decks or mark cards during online poker, yet there are a few effective online poker cheating techniques.

- ***Collusion.*** Secretly colluding online is even easier. Simply sign onto the same online poker service and sit down at the same table. Hang out together in the same room with your laptops and look at each other's hands, or simply talk on the phone during the hands and discuss.
- ***Bots.*** These are programs that play for you using statistical analyses. Sometimes these win; sometimes they don't, as poker is not an exact science like chess.

- *Sudden Disconnect.* Most online poker sites offer protection in case one's computer disconnects during the hand. In these cases, the player remains in the hand, but he can no longer bet, as if he were all-in. You can take advantage of this when you are in a hand that you no longer want to bet on. Simply unplug and let the hand play out to see if you've won.

15. Beat the Dice

I know a guy who was so furious with a casino that he hooked up a catheter to his schlong, hid the tube beneath his pants, and while playing craps, urinated on the casino floor undetected. He still lost, but perhaps he felt some sort of vindication. Truth is, it's the casinos that are pissing on us. And the only good way to get back at them is to take *their* money. Here are more lucrative ways to gety our revenge while playing dice.

Loaded Dice

Buy a pair of dice from the casino gift shop and learn how to alter them. Creating trick dice is like a fun project and can be a great advantage in an unmonitored game, such as street dice or a friendly game among acquaintances

- ***Alter the Weight.*** Add weight or remove weight in particular areas of the dice so that they land how you want them.
- ***Alter the Face.*** Alter an edge or the face to have them land as you wish.

"Borrowing" Chips

At the casino, if you are running a little low on chips, you can help yourself to your neighbor's. The best time to do this is

15. Better that the chips go to you than some slimy casino.

when it is their turn to shoot the dice and they are preoccupied. Whether or not you want to return the chips after you've borrowed them is up to you.

Befriend a Croupier

These guys are whip smart when it comes to the craps payouts, and they are good to have on your side. Ways to get them in your corner is, obviously, conspiring to give them half of the take or to ply them with prostitutes.

Find a Buddy

If you can, find an accomplice to work the table with you. He or she can distract other players while you take your loan from them. He could also distract croupiers while you add chips atop your winning stack after the roll has completed.

Practice Roll

Practice rolling your dice by pairing them up in the numbers that you want, and then rolling them so that there is very little rotation and the numbers remain face up. Some hard workers get good enough with their dice to bank them and come up with the numbers they want. If you want, make your practice just like a real craps table. You can actually buy one at a casino supply store or from a casino.

16. Avoid Cleaning Up After Your Dog

Unless you stop feeding it, the shit never stops. A dog that lives 15 years will require you to pick up almost 11,000 shits—an impossible task—which is why it is so important to use some of the tactics outlined below.

A cautionary tale: A relative of mine once let her dog crap on somebody's lawn and she didn't clean it up or hide it. She just left the steaming load there and went on home. A few minutes later her doorbell rang. She answered the door, and a woman was holding a gardening spade willed with warm dog feces. The woman flung the shit in my relative's face, while shouting, "Next time, clean it up!" An understandable reaction and one that you should employ if somebody lets their dog crap on *your* lawn.

Night time is the right time . . . When you walk your dog under the cover of darkness, late night or early morning, you have more flexibility during the load removal process. If nobody is around (or peering at you from a window), then you can just quietly walk away without detection.

Scooper-fake. If people are present but inattentive to your dog's feat on the neighbor's lawn, then you can pull off the Scooper-Fake or the Undercover Sting. Lean over and pretend to remove the poop for about ten seconds, and then continue walking.

The cover-up. Cover up the feces by tossing some discarded branches, leaves, grass tufts, granite, or rocks on top of the poop mound.

Go abroad. If your dog has already been labeled the neighborhood crapper, then you may be under too much scrutiny to pull off these previous methods. So you may have to take your dog's business somewhere else. Find a secluded spot in the area for your dog to use as his toilet. It could be behind a public building, in an alleyway, in a wooded area, in a quiet

16. Your shit-eating dog will eliminate the hassle of cleaning up after her plus save you money on dog food.

region of a different neighborhood, anyplace without spectators.

The nut job. If people fear your unpredictable rages, then they will leave you and your dog alone—it won't matter that you aren't cleaning up after your dog. People will just be relieved that you aren't picking up the poop and smearing it on your face before you begin a ritual dance.

Buried alive. Carry a bag of dirt or gravel with you when you walk your dog. After the pup finishes his business, just sprinkle the spot and move on. If you are kind enough to consider picking up after your crap machine, then this is a perfect primer step to make the poop clump before you scoop it.

Train a shit-eater. Every dog has shit-eating potential; their skills just need to be honed. Encourage your dog, when he attempts to eat his own waste, and he will gladly begin to develop the habit. Eventually, your dog will be conditioned to vacuum up his own messes on walks.

17. Get Free Internet

The Internet knows no borders, shows no bias, and has no limits. It's all about sharing—built by all of us—for all of us. That's precisely why Internet zillionaires shouldn't mind sharing a little back. Having to pay $50 a month for the rest of your life for something we all are supposed to share is like being shaken down by the mob. (See chapter 26, "Join the Mafia.") You need to stand up to these dot-com dickheads. Here are methods by which to secure free Internet service.

Promotion Hunting

Many Internet service providers offer free Internet as promotions to entice you to enroll in their company, buy their products, or look at their banner advertisements. Simply jump from Internet service to Internet service until your free time periods run out. Companies such as AOL, Net Zero, and Juno are known to offer these promotions. You can also visit The Free Site (thefreesite.com) to get additional links for free or low-cost ISPs. Just make sure you opt out before the provider automatically enrolls you in their program and begins charging you fees.

"Share" Your Neighbor's Signal

Just get on your laptop and search for a neighboring unprotected wireless signal and begin borrowing it. The argument can be made that his or her signal is actually invading your property and, therefore, it is yours to use; you're just protecting your land. If the only connection you can find is secure, you can even learn how to crack the code with software at Aircracking-ng.com. If this makes you uncomfortable, you can also strike a deal with your neighbor, and, in exchange for the connection, agree to do a few tasks for her such as making household repairs, picking a few weeds, or digging her car out of the snow. If you simply want a discount, simply ask if she'd be interested in splitting the fee in half.

17. Parlay your free Internet into online poker winnings by colluding with a friend who is playing at the same virtual poker table. (See chapter 14, "Cheat at Poker."

Hot Spot Hunting

Visit Wi-Fi hot spots at coffee houses, libraries, restaurants, hotels, malls—places that don't require you to purchase anything—and do all of your Internet work on the road. Consider yourself an Internet social butterfly. This method requires you to have a wireless network adapter. If you can't get the signal, ask the cashier or receptionist for the user name and password, and he or she will usually give it to you.

18. Hot-Wire a Car

Remember all the controversy surrounding the video game Grand Theft Auto? People ranted that it was too violent and that it encouraged criminal behavior. But the real problem is that the game doesn't even teach you how to properly steal a car. Children are being taken advantage of and spending their coveted allowance on a game with a deceiving title. Stand up for kids everywhere and teach them the basics of auto theft with the information herein.

Warning

Understand that there is a risk of electrical shock in this process, and there is a chance that you will encounter a kill-switch, which will prevent you from successfully completing the hot-wire.

1. *Open the hood and locate the positive side of the coil wire, which is red.* The coil wire is connected to the plug wires, so you can find it by tracing the plug wires to the red coil wire. (It can be found at the back of the engine on V-8 engine cars; in the left center on 6-cylinder cars; and in the right center on 4-cylinder cars.)
2. *Supply the dash with power by running an additional wire from the positive side of the battery to the positive red coil wire.* The dashboard needs power before the car is able to run.

3. *Cross the positive battery cable with the wire next to it called the starter solenoid.* The solenoid uses electromagnetic force to distribute power to the starter. It will usually be mounted on top of the starter, but it may be on the fender near the battery on some Ford models. Use a screwdriver or pliers to cross the two cables. Successfully crossing them revs the engine. (Make sure the car is in a stable position once the cables have been crossed. If it is an automatic, then it should be in park. If it is a manual transmission, then it should be in neutral with the parking brake on.)
4. *Unlock the steering wheel.* Insert a flathead screwdriver between the steering wheel and the steering column. Push against the column, and forcefully push the locking pin away from the wheel.

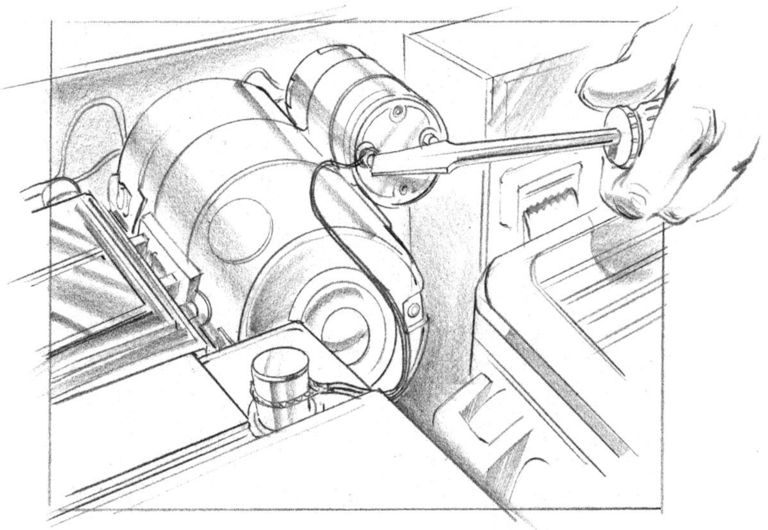

18. Dazzle your friends by hot-wiring a car. One step is to cross the positive battery cable with the starter solenoid wire.

LEGENDS OF BAD

Liam Moynihan

Liam Moynihan enjoyed driving, especially in a beautiful region like the Puget Sound of Seattle. But like anyone will tell you, driving the same car for more than a few hours simply gets tiresome. So, to liven up his scenic jaunts around the Sound, using only a hammer and screwdriver, Moynihan hot-wired 136 cars in a six-month period, a spellbinding pace of one stolen car every thirty-two hours. His favorite cars to steal were Hondas and Subarus, perhaps due to their reliability.

19. Fake Your Own Death

A tiresome wife, irritating kids, sickly dog, mortgage payments, an intense boss, insufferable coworkers . . . if you're dead all of it goes away. And, if you really want to make people feel horrible, you can have them believe that they were personally responsible for your death. Your stepmother just punished you for something innocuous, like sneaking out of your bedroom. Now, you've decided to repay her, and your father for marrying her, by committing suicide in their name. Leave them with a suicide e-mail (make sure to cc everyone in the world, and include a link to a dark, twisted YouTube rant about how unfair they were toward you).

How will you die? Will it be a suicide? Were you murdered? Victim of a random act of violence or an accident?

Suicide

This is difficult because it requires witnesses—and a spectacle. You only have a few suicide options that eliminate the need for a discovered body. Bridge-jumping is ideal. You must know how to survive a fall from a bridge or a high altitude, bring a source of oxygen to keep you alive during your swim away from the scene, and wear a wetsuit under your clothes so you don't freeze during the getaway swim. Practice the bridge-jumping technique on smaller, more private bridges, so that you are ready for your big performance. On the day of your death, make sure you attract the attention of passersby by standing on the ledge and shouting about "how sorry they will be when you end it all." Let people see your face, and maybe throw your name into a few rants ("This is the last time they'll push John Smith around"). Once everyone has seen you—and heard enough to identify you to a policeman later—you are ready to jump.

Murder

Murder must be methodically planned, because you don't want to leave any messes that point to an innocent person as the murder suspect. Try a "vacation murder." Tell people that you just need to get away, and take a vacation by yourself. Many countries, such as Haiti, will issue death certificates for bribes of a few hundred dollars. Make sure that the certificate is mailed to the proper family members, and walk cleanly away from your life.

Random Act of Violence

Spread the word that you just acquired a new watch, new rims for your car, or any material possession that may attract thieves. Make a trip to a part of town that is considered "seedy" or "dangerous," and set one of two plans in action:

- ***The homicide carjacking:*** While you are on a deserted stretch of road, discard your car's rims, stereo, your valuables, and your wallet. Once this has been accomplished, smash your driver-side window and smear blood on the driver's seat and on the steering wheel. Flick some of the blood against the dashboard, the passenger seat and window, and the windshield (on the inside) to create a spatter pattern. The object is to attribute your death to a gunshot or blunt trauma force. If you want to go the extra mile, leave a tooth behind.

Once you have finished creating the crime scene, call 911 and express an incoherent panic to the operator. As long as it is clear that you are being robbed by strangers and you fear that your life is in danger, then you are ready to hang up the phone, make your escape, and begin your new life.

- *The fiery carjacking:* Follow the same steps listed above, but after creating a gruesome murder scene, you will burn it. The ideal method of carrying out this plan involves finding a corpse that resembles you. If you can't obtain a corpse, then you will have to improvise. Smear and spatter blood, leave an article of clothing in the car, leave the keys in the ignition, and discard all of your valuables. When you make the 911 call, sound weakened and disoriented, and tell the operator that the thieves have stolen your belongings and your car. Douse the car with gasoline, light it on fire, and disappear.

You've Been Kidnapped

Disappear for a few days, and hide in a remote location. Use a local pay phone to make a single phone call to one of your relatives. You can either assume the role of the deadly kidnapper and demand a ransom, or use your own (distraught) voice to explain that you have been kidnapped (and your kidnapper requires an exorbitant sum of money before he releases you). After the phone call, you are free to begin a new life while your relatives assume the worst.

The Swimming or Boating Accident

Go to a lake or ocean to spend time by yourself, but make sure that your family knows where you are. If you are going to fake a drowning, then leave your car parked near the body of water, and escape by using a getaway car that you stashed

19. A fake kidnapping is a great way to start over.

near the location. Leave a single garment, like a towel on the beach or a pair of goggles on the shoreline, which your loved ones will identify as yours. When your car doesn't move for a few days, your family will begin to realize that you never made it out of the water. If you are going to stage a boating accident, then follow the aforementioned steps, but include a capsized boat and a floating bag or cooler in the equation. (Don't try to give clues to your family that you might not make it back from the water. If anything, you want to appear *too* confident; you are in no danger as you go out on the water by yourself.)

Deadly Serendipity

If you are lucky enough to experience a natural disaster in your area, then get close to the epicenter of the destruction and throw some of your belongings with identification into the rubble. As workers sift through it to look for remains, they will count you among the dead.

How to Begin a New Life

- *Go to the Social Security Administration* and tell them that you are the victim of harrassment or violence (you must provide proof). Ask them to aid you by assigning you a new social security number. Relocate and begin a new life with a new name. You still may use one of the death-feigning tricks for fun, but they are not necessary when you enlist the government's help.
- *Sever all ties to your past friends, family, coworkers, and life-style.* If you are finding a new identity on your own (without government assistance), then you will have to resort to shady Internet identification dealers or paper tripping, or you could become a shape-shifting name changer.
- ***Internet Deals:*** There are plenty of fake ID sources on the Internet, in studio apartments in Chinatown, in the basement of a guy who knows a guy, in the storage rooms of printing presses, and so on. Find a connection and make sure you can trust your fake ID source. Inspect the quality of the IDs in person before you commit to anything, and never let anyone know your real name. Research your new identity to make sure that you are not a wanted felon. Use your new ID with discretion. If

you are using a fake ID, you may want to work off the books, stay away from tax forms, and avoid opening up too many credit card accounts.

- *Paper Tripping:* Paper trippers search graveyards for names of dead people who share their year of birth. They make counterfeit birth certificates with those names, and then they use the birth certificates to obtain driver's licenses. (When you obtain your new driver's license, do it in a state that has minimal ID requirements.)
- *Shape-shifting:* You could live life under a series of aliases and become a remorseless con-man after you fake your death. This saves you the trouble of finding documentation, a steady job, or even a new home.

LEGENDS OF BAD

Timothy Dexter

Before Timothy Dexter faked his own death, he was already on a legendary course. While some people play dead for financial gain, Dexter, a notoriously uneducated man, had amassed a fortune in a series of business deals that were deemed by the elite to be outrageously stupid, yet netted him enormous wealth. (For example, in the 1780s, he invested in depreciated Continental currency that soon skyrocketed; he also sold stray cats to the Caribbean Islands.) But then his wife began nagging him a little too hard. Dexter soon wondered how she'd react if he had died. So he faked his own death. At his funeral, Dexter watched furiously when his wife didn't cry at his passing. So he did what any normal husband would do, and he came back to life just so he could cane her. Repeatedly.

20. Carry on an Affair

When guys give their women the "we're programmed to spread our seed" argument, some women will come back with their penguins theory—that they are mammals that live their entire lives with just one partner. But you're smarter than a penguin, and you're taller than a penguin, and you're stronger than a penguin. So screw penguins.

Sure, you want to remain faithful, so for sexual variety, you turn to Internet porn. But then when a smutty pop-up ad hits while your five-year-old daughter is playing on kidz.com, her innocence is lost forever, and your wife never forgives you for it. So you are forced to step up, be a man, and blame the porn on your son. Yet this can create years of unresolved tension between father and son. So if you're a true family man, you do what's best for your family by having an affair.

Be Smart

An affair does not always connote "love affair." The easily concealed affairs are those between strangers who have no connections outside of their hotel room. When you cheat with the secretary, you will likely be caught. When you cheat with your sister-in-law, you will likely be caught and possibly subjected to a brawl. The perfect affair finds equilibrium between pragmatism and passion. The actual sex is new and suffused with passion (that's the point), but when your pants are on, you and your affair partner are still complicit in a clandestine act of roguery.

Determine what you are looking to gain from this affair. If it is just sex, then establish the ground rules up front: "Sex, no strings." Make sure your partner agrees to those rules before anything begins.

The Ideal Partner

The ideal partner is a hot stranger with no links to your life. You may even want him or her to be someone who irks you in order to prevent the onset of a love affair, which can get sloppy. If your affair partner is single and uninterested in involvement, then they are ideal. Unfortunately, few people fit this description. Most single people develop an interest in involvement. You should always make sure that your affair partner has as much or more to lose than you do (to avoid complications upon the termination of the affair). Therefore, it may be wiser to have an affair with another married or romantically involved person. If you have two kids, then they should have three. Of course, the affair partner's spouse could pose some danger to the relationship—or to your body—so brief your partner on the spouse-deception techniques that you plan to use.

Sage Advice

- *Never call your affair partner from your home phone, work phone, or personal cellular phone.* Open up a second cellular account (maybe even under an alias), and call them from that phone.
- *Do not use personal e-mail.* If you open up an alternate e-mail account through which you plan to communicate with your girlfriend or boyfriend, then do not access that account from your home computer, personal cell phone, or any other device that your spouse may access.

Use a public computer such as a community library or Internet cafe (but make sure you are not being tailed by a P.I.) or a private computer or laptop that only you can access. If your spouse is spying on you using computer monitoring software, then he or she will be able to trace your indiscretions even if you delete your surfing history, use a private e-mail account, and hide or delete your files. You may want to use privacy software to preclude the possibility of being caught.

- *Do not put your "affair expenses" on any shared credit cards.* Open up a separate credit card account for such discretionary spending. This is a card that your spouse should not know about, so keep it away from your other cards. Do not hide it in the sock drawer either, though, because you do not want to do anything secretive enough to arouse suspicion.
- *Open up a P.O. Box* where your credit card statements and second phone bills can be sent.
- *Do not leave a paper trail.* If you buy a Valentine's gift that your spouse never receives, and a P.I. uncovers that credit card statement, then you're screwed. Use cash, and the world will forget that you were ever there. Never save any receipts!
- *Do not use local hotels or restaurants.* You may even want to go out of state to meet your affair partner, so maybe you can play the old "business trip" card and keep your meetings infrequent.
- *Never visit the same hotel or restaurant more than once.* You do not want to be identified as a "regular" at a bar with someone other than your spouse.
- When you have a scheduled date, do not travel together to your intended destination. *You should never be in the same car as your affair partner,* because an accident or an observant acquaintance will expose your secret. You

should also avoid checking into the hotel together. Book separate rooms beforehand, and rendezvous in one room after your separate check-ins. (If you are able to book the rooms under pseudonyms—see chapter 6: "Get an Alias"—then that would be ideal.)

Life with Your Spouse

- *Do not tell anyone about the affair.* You cannot even confide in your best friend. Do not even think about recording the details of the affair in a journal or a blog. Come on. Your affair partner must agree to the same code of secrecy.
- *Keep your routines consistent.* Do not abandon your spouse or family to be with your affair partner. Do not contact your affair partner when you are at home or anywhere within view of your spouse. When you and your affair partner have a date, it should fall in a window of time during which you would normally be out of the house.
- *Feign interest in your spouse and the banalities of family life.* Listen to your spouse's stories, have spontaneous dinners every once in a while, plan vacations with verve, and do not stop having sex with your spouse.

However . . .

- *Do not become overly affectionate or overly withdrawn when you are with your spouse.* Often, love for one's spouse and the guilt of the affair drive one to act erratically. Do not overcompensate by buying your spouse gifts, taking extravagant trips, or punctuating every syllable with "I Love You" (unless this is already your established routine). Conversely, do not avoid conversations with your spouse, cancel plans, or behave irascibly during family time. Do not check your watch or act as though you have somewhere better to be. Some of these behaviors are unconscious symptoms of a cheater, so be aware of your body language and actual language at all times.

20. It's important to work as hard on your affairs as you do on your marriage. Don't travel with your partner in the same car and never visit the same hotel twice.

- *Do not become obsessed with your appearance.* This can include vain extremes like waxing areas that had never been waxed before or restyling your hair and wardrobe. But it also includes trivial modifications like new accessories, new underwear, an extra ten hours at the gym per week, and so on. These alterations to your appearance will become red flags to your spouse. If you truly have resolved to change something about your appearance, then talk to your spouse about your desire to do so *beforehand,* and convince him or her that the change is for you (or your spouse).

The Relationship with Your Affair Partner

- *Meet infrequently.* The meetings should be planned well in advance so that you can concoct an alibi to feed your spouse.
- *Try to maintain a regular schedule of dates.* Do not arrange impromptu trysts, because impulsive behavior will tip off your spouse.
- *Avoid pillow talk or intimate bonding.* Part of the beauty of booking separate hotel rooms is the option to *sleep* in separate hotel rooms after the deed is done.
- *Never use pet names or lovey-dovey language when you speak to your affair partner.* This can segue into romance, which is dangerous territory.
- *Keep phone conversations and e-mail exchanges minimal.* Ideally, you will plan your next rendezvous when you are wrapping up the present one, which will remove any need to communicate by phone or e-mail.
- *Do not keep any mementoes of the affair.* Bring a change of clothes to the hotel and shower thoroughly before you go home, because you do not want to exude a tell-tale sex smell (or smell like someone else's perfume or cologne).

- *Keep spending to a minimum.* You do not want your affair partner to expect lavish meals or gifts from you, because things could turn sour when you stop providing.
- *When it is time to end the affair, do so kindly but firmly.* Do not act like a weasel when it is over, because you do not want your partner informing your spouse of your secret life. If you chose your affair partner wisely, it should be relatively easy to end it.

(If you suspect that a P.I. is tailing you, then refer to chapter 10, "Evade Surveillance.")

21. Score Free Food

The good Bible tells us that God created all sorts of foods to eat for all, yet nowhere is there any mention of having to pay for any of it. This chapter does not include the common "dine and dash" technique because that is outright stealing from a waiter's pocket. This doesn't mean you cannot tell a hostess that it's your friend's birthday, in order to earn some free after-dinner cake. Just make sure you don't let the wait staff skate by without having to reluctantly sing "Happy Birthday" in unison.

Free Snacks

- *Work the free sample circuit at the local mall or grocery store.* You may be lucky enough to find actual free sample booths, but even if nobody is voluntarily handing out samples, you can request them. Go to the fast-food counters with buffet layouts, and ask them to sample a few items before you place your order. After you eat the samples, tell them that nothing really appeals to you and move on to the next place. Ask for samples of cheese, meat, or any of the side dishes on display in the butcher section of the grocery store to "aid in your decision." Turn grapes, cherries, salad bar items, bakery items, or nuts and granola from the dispensers into free nibbles at the grocery store as you carry on your free sample pilgrimage.

21. Help them market their products by accepting their free food.

- *Locate berries, plants, and nuts that are indigenous to your region, and snack on them throughout the seasons.* Ask around to find out which foods commonly grow in the area, and seek out the appropriate trees and bushes. Black walnut trees leave a spattering of edible nuts throughout many regions of the country—the South, Northeast, and the more temperate Western states. Just collect the green-husked nuts as you walk around town, and do the work later to extract the meat. You can even offer to remove the black walnuts from your neighbors' yards in order to collect more of them—you may be able to earn a small income scoring this free food. Raspberries, blackberries, and blueberries often grow wild in rural regions and even along the sides of roads. Crab apple trees are also prevalent in public areas. There are a number of plants that are edible, such as dandelions, pokeweeds, sassafras, thistle, daylilies, and cattails.

Speak to local botanists and learn how to convert wildlife into delicious snacks or even a light dinner.

- *Go to a fancy restaurant and tell the waiter that you are meeting a friend.* Fill up on free bread, then hastily beckon the waiter and tell him that your friend has been in an accident, and you will have to leave abruptly. In the midst of your dramatic performance, offer to pay for the bread; after the waiter refuses to charge you for the bread, walk away with a gut of gratis dough.
- *Off to college:* Locate the local office buildings and campus cafeterias with minimum security and maximum buffet fare. Scantily fill a bowl with food (or fill it liberally depending on how much you are willing to risk) and approach the cashier. Invent a story about leaving your money in the office or dorm room, car, or executive sauna, and fill out an IOU. This only works once, so no repeat appearances.

Meals

- *Create a stolen garden.* Set aside a patch of your lawn or a window box for food plants. Pocket a few plant seeds—or more brazen rogues may pocket a few young vegetable plants—from your local nursery, and plant them in your own garden. Ask friends if you can snip parts of their vegetable plants and transplant them into your garden. Soon you will have an arsenal of salad ingredients for which you only paid the price of mulch. The amoral advice would be to outright steal your neighbors' plants and then spread a rumor that the deer and gophers are hungrier than ever before. But roguery does not endorse profiting from innocent people's losses.
- *Play the irate customer card.* You need to have a strong stomach to mold yourself into one of those irritating

people who find fault in everything and demand refunds and free gifts of appeasement. But those people don't spend much money. If you are eating at a restaurant, insist on seeing the manager to complain about the food (not the service) halfway through the meal. Tell them that it tastes stale, the sauce is salty, the pasta is undercooked—anything that would elicit an apology from the manager. The goal is to make him apologetic enough to offer to erase the bill. If he initially offers to send it back, tell him that you have already eaten too much of it, and you don't want anyone to have to cook an extra meal; or, the more obnoxious answer would be: I don't trust them to cook anything else. Be tactful. You want to seem displeased, but you do not want to be confrontational, because the manager will not be inclined to placate a total jerk.

Join the Party

- *Walk into heavily populated backyard barbeques and eat a few burgers* while you mingle with the strangers. Tell everyone that you are with John.
- *Sit in on catered meetings in conference centers at work* (it doesn't always have to be *your* office—scope out the corporate scene and see whose employees always have the heartiest sauce stains on their shirts in the afternoon; then, acquire a copy of their meeting schedule). At school, universities always have catered events taking place.
- *Scoop up the goods at reunions and receptions in hotels and banquet halls.* Always have your fake identity in mind when you attend these events. If people start asking questions, you want to have answers to satisfy, baffle, or disgust them enough to make them leave you alone.

- This option may be a little creepy, but you could *work the Chuck E. Cheese* scene. Kids' parties always have unguarded cake and pizza, and there are always new parents present that nobody has ever met. You are Kaitlin's reclusive mom who plans "to leave right after this slice of pizza . . . sorry we didn't get a chance to talk earlier."

Free Bonuses

Happy Birthday, 365: Join restaurant and frequent shopper clubs, and record a different birthday for each application. Keep track of which birthday will be celebrated at which location, and reap the benefits of your eternal day of celebration. Many restaurants offer free food to their members on their birthdays, and certain stores will provide discounts and free merchandise.

22. Mask Marijuana Smoke

Realize how much time we've lost worrying about the smell of pot smoke. What other classic songs would the Beatles or Men Without Hats have composed with that time back? The Native Americans didn't have to spend any time thinking about masking the smoke, and they had something like twenty gods—far more productive than our religious moralists who have conjured up only one.

The Basics

- Try to *find a private space* that will not be too populated throughout the day.
- Once you have sequestered yourself inside of a room, *use a damp towel to seal the space under the door.*
- *Cover your hair* with a hat, or, if you have longer hair, tie it back.
- *Open windows* and turn on a fan before you light up.
- Position yourself to *smoke out of the window* (to ensure that the smoke is not seeping into any other rooms in the building, close the other windows in the building).
- When you are finished smoking, *change your clothes, brush your teeth (or chew gum),* and use whatever measures you normally use to diminish redness of the eyes.

Rub a little scented mousse into your hair and remove any hats or head coverings.

- Your *smoking clothes should be placed into a hamper or a sealed bag* immediately.
- *Let the candles or incense burn* while the room continues to air out. When you are prepared to leave the room, rub a little scented oil on your neck.

The Spoof Method

Many people smoke using a spoof, or a cardboard tube from a roll of paper towels with a dryer sheet attached to one end. The dryer sheet acts as a freshening filter. You inhale, pick up the spoof, and exhale into the tube. This does not guarantee that the smoke will be completely masked by fresh mountain scent—it just takes a bit of the edge off of the smoke.

Hold the spoof out the window, and make sure that the fan is blowing the smoke away from the house. If you have curtains, tie them up above the window frame with twine or ribbon so that they don't retain the smell of the smoke. Try to protect exposed fabric in the room from direct contact with the smoke.

Masking Scents

- ***Incense:*** Do not choose an overwhelming incense fragrance—sandalwood, patchouli, jasmine, or another woody scent is perfect. Do not burn french vanilla or something unnatural, because it will not blend with the pot smoke as well.
- ***Aromatherapy Oil:*** This gives off a potent, but usually enjoyable fragrance. Again, go with organic scents.
- ***Scented Candles:*** These are not strongly recommended, but Glade oil candles are effective if you choose the proper scent. Angel whispers or spiced rose and vanilla

22. The Spoof method: paper towel roll plus fabric softener.

are the best. Do not use any food, cinnamon, or floral-scented candles.

- ***Perfumes and Colognes:*** Do not use perfume or cologne, because it only gives the wafts of marijuana smoke more pungency. You do not want to stomp out the smoke smell; rather, you want to create a blend of aromas that work in harmony with the smoke. If you insist on using a spray, use a hemp spray or a natural deodorizer.
- ***Spray Air Freshener:*** Forbidden for the reasons stated above.

23. Siphon Gas

Want to get gallons and gallons of gasoline for free? Just go to an auto junkyard and siphon some out. But sadly, sometimes you don't even have enough fuel to get out to a junkyard, and you must stop over at a mall or hospital parking lot to source your gas. Find a spot, and then wait for a car to park. Watch the occupants head inside and you should have plenty of time to borrow what you need in order to get to your next destination. If you have a guilty conscience, target a Porsche—these guys have money to burn, and if they don't then they shouldn't have a Porsche in the first place.

Quick Method: The Suck Up

1. *Place a length of clear plastic tubing*, or if resources are minimal, a straw, into the gas tank, and submerge it below the surface level of the gasoline.
2. *Blow into it* to ensure that you have hit the gas. If you hear bubbles, then you are in. If your straw comes into contact with anything solid, then try to insert it from a different angle.
3. *Extract the tube and check the rim* to make sure that it has come in contact with the gasoline, then reinsert it and begin sucking.
4. *Spit the gas into a bucket.*

5. Once the bucket is full enough, take it to your car, *place a funnel in your tank opening,* and pour the new gas inside.

Expert Method: The Craftsman

1. *Create a seven-foot hose* using clear plastic tubing.
2. *Insert the hose into the gas tank,* and submerge the end of it under the surface level of the gas. To ensure that the hose is under the surface level, blow into the free end of the hose and listen for bubbles in the tank.
3. *Create a U with the hose.* Let the hose droop from the tank to the ground, then loop back up to elevate the free end of the hose above the surface level of the gas in the tank.
4. *Suck the gas.*
5. You will notice that *the gas drains down one side of the U* and stops at gas tank surface level on the other side of the U. The gas will remain at that level in the hose until you bring the free end down below gas tank surface level.
6. While the free end of the hose is still elevated, *grab a bucket and insert the end* into it.
7. Slowly lower the hose below gas-tank surface level, and *allow the gas to drain into the bucket.*
8. When you have enough gas, *lift the hose up into the air to straighten it* (you may need a chair or a step ladder), and the gas will flow back into the tank.

Anti-Siphon

Many modern cars are designed to deter gas siphoning. There are anti-siphon devices and anti-rollover devices in place that

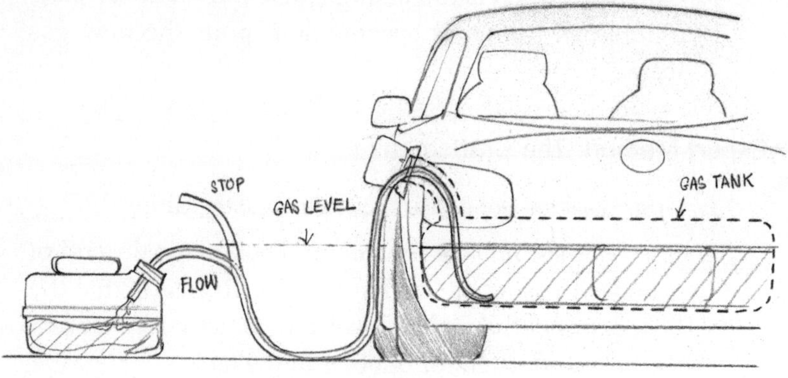

23. The price of gas has never been lower.

prevent gas leaks in the event of an accident. You may be able to remove the anti-rollover device, but you would be increasing the risk of fire if that car gets into an accident. If your hose continually meets with resistance when you try the procedures above, then you may be working with an anti-siphon device.

There are a few ways to get around the anti-siphon device, but none of them are foolproof. They all depend on how resilient the car is and how adept you are at handy work.

1. *Remove the gas tank* and remove the fill tube for the gas. Set the tank on a stool or something elevated, and tip the tank to the side to make the gas run out through the fill tube opening.
2. *Disconnect the engine gas-supply hose* exiting the gas tank. Place the end of the hose in a bucket, then find the fuel pump fuse box under the hood on the driver's side. Using the fuel pump switch wires, turn on the fuel pump, and the gas will pump into the bucket.

LEGENDS OF BAD

Chad Storey

If the siphoning techniques featured in this chapter are considered introductory, this cheap-ass dude offered a graduate level course in the subject. Chad Storey had a switch installed behind his dash which activated a hose that would suck gas from another car's fuel tank and transfer it directly into his own tank. As he sat comfortably in the big cushy driver's seat of his gas-guzzling Dodge Ram truck, it would take a mere six to eight minutes to fill his entire twenty-gallon fuel tank. Then, one day, as Storey was standing beside a blue minivan, looking pretty sketchy and reeking of gas, he got nabbed by the cops. However, the police were "extremely impressed by the ingenuity" of Storey's elaborate siphoning system.

24. Cheat on Tests

Learning how to analyze the subtleties of *Beowulf* or how to decipher the cosine of a trapezoid might be considered essential by some educators, but nothing you'll learn throughout the course of your schooling is as vital as learning how to pass tests. This chapter offers a multitude of ways one can solve the problem of not being prepared enough or intelligent enough to pass the tests that educators thrust upon us. Though having a well-rounded education sounds nice, you are better off spending your study time truly focusing on the subjects that you excel at or are most interested in—having a narrow but sharpened expertise will better serve you in the future. Most importantly, you should be spending your time socializing with other students to nurture your intrapersonal skills—the skills you'll need when networking for a job later in life. Other such skills include playing beer pong, smoking spliffs (see chapter 22, "Mask Marijuana Smoke"), and tag teaming.

First, you need to outline your teacher's methodology. Do they disseminate the same test to all classes? Do they alter each class's tests? Do they rock the scantron? Does everyone in the class receive identical answer sheets or do they vary by student? By row?

Uniform Tests

The easiest method to overcome is the uniform test method. This is rare, but some teachers distribute the same copy of a test to every class.

- Simply *form a chain of cheaters* connected to an A student in the teacher's earliest class. The student will take the test, ace it, and pass the answers on to the slackers.
- If the test is too long for a person to memorize, then *the first person in the chain takes a covert picture of each page with a camera phone,* and he passes it on to his fellow cheaters via e-mail or text.
- The first person pulls the old "I didn't get a test" gimmick, convincing the teacher that he or she miscounted the number of people in the row, while he pockets the original copy of the test. The cheaters later *study the original copy of the test* and research and memorize the correct answers.

The Mechanical Pencil

Make an answer sheet or a cheat sheet on a small piece of paper, then roll up that paper, insert it in the lead slot of a mechanical pencil, and bring that pencil to the test with you. Answer the questions you know first, and then pretend to add lead to your pencil and discretely read the answers on the sheet.

The extra pencil. Write cheat sheet answers on a second No. 2 pencil and place it on your desk.

The teacher's edition. If you can determine that the teacher gives tests right out of the book, then buy the teacher's edition and cheat on tests, quizzes, and homework assignments.

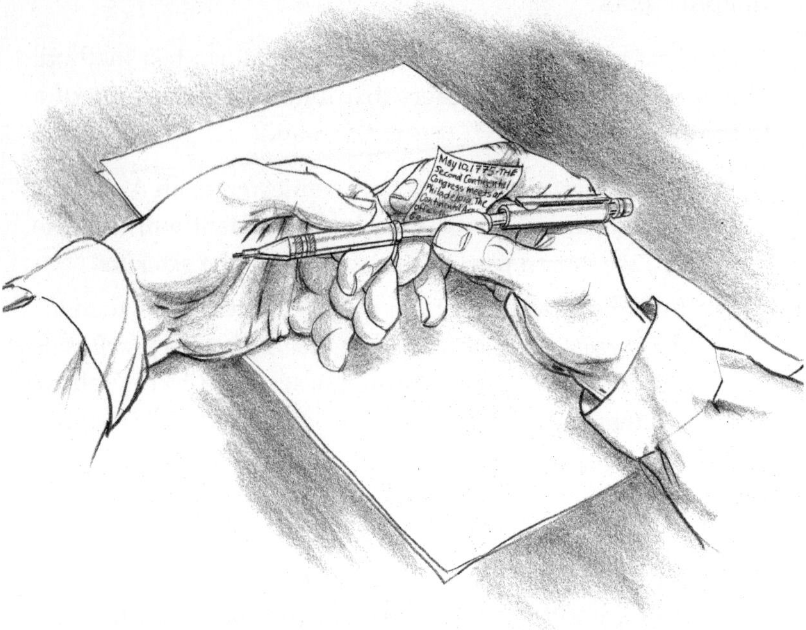

24. Place a rolled cheat sheet inside your mechanical pencil. Act like you are refilling the lead, then access your answers.

The eraser. Bring a rubber: Cut into an eraser (not enough to snap it) and peel it up to reveal the middle. Write a cheat sheet on that center pulp, and then place the flap back down; allowing the eraser to resume its original shape (you can do this on both sides). During the test, make it seem like you are tinkering with the eraser due to some nervous tick. Every time you flick the flap of the eraser, memorize the answers inside.

The toilet tank. Get tanked: Tape an answer sheet to the bottom of the toilet tank lid or the uppermost region of the interior of the toilet tank (above the water line). Go to the bathroom during the test and look at the answers.

Cheat sheets. The cheat-sheet method works with Coke bottles, bracelets, rubber bands, ski-pass holders on jackets, skin, the undersides of fingernails, scrap paper, clothing, the soles of shoes, the insides of pens, book covers, and so on.

Footsie. Make a deal to cheat with a smarter classmate, and establish a code of foot signals that they can use to communicate the answers.

The calculator. If you have an advanced calculator, you can make a deal with a smarter classmate. They record their answers in code (a = 1, b = 2, therefore 12342312 = abcdbcab to the first 8 questions). Then you ask the teacher if you can borrow that student's calculator toward the end of the test. You need a good reason (your calculator doesn't seem to be working, they are sitting right next to you, you are only familiar with the commands on that calculator brand) to convince the teacher.

Get Excused During the Test

- Halfway through the test *become sick* and request to finish the test the next day.
- Plan to *have yourself "suddenly" called out of class* during the test (you need co-conspirators on this one).

Don't Turn In the Test

- Take it home with you, study it, and *never bring it back.* When the teacher claims that you never handed it in, convince him that it must have been lost and ask to take it again.
- Take it home with you, fill in the answers (get one wrong for credence's sake), and correct it by emulating the teacher's style (curve of X's and check marks, exclamation points after praise, and so on), handwriting, and pen color. When the teacher says that they do not have a grade for you later in the semester, *show them the marked test* as proof that you took it, and it was graded.

Plagiarism Methods

Paraphrase. Find numerous sources and create a paraphrased amalgam of all of them. Do not paraphrase any single source for more than two consistent sentences. If you are writing about the history of New York, intersperse details from each of the sources into every paragraph.

A hired quill. Pay someone to write your paper for you, but do not purchase prewritten papers online. If you are going to plagiarize responsibly, you need to know the guidelines of the writing assignment and the specific topic before you assign someone the task of writing it. Give your teacher's criteria to the hired writer, and proofread the paper to make sure that it falls within the parameters of the assignment.

Paraphrase the teacher. (This method is usually restricted to high school and introductory college courses.) Write down some of the teacher's direct quotes during lectures or discussions, artfully rephrase them while keeping the meaning intact, and make them the pillars of your essay. Your teacher will be so happy to see a paper structured around such an insightful—yet familiar—thesis statement.

Paraphrase a vocal classmate. Same method as above. Select the classmate wisely. You do not want to paraphrase a windbag or an idiot, so make sure that your chosen classmate impresses the teacher when he or she speaks.

LEGENDS OF BAD

Timothy Barrus

Timothy Barrus is a Michigan-born writer who began his career by writing gay erotica and sadomasochistic novels. Naturally, his early work left him yearning for a transition into the Native American memoir genre. However, he was faced with one complication: he had no Native American identity or life experience from which he could find inspiration for his artistic impulse. Most authors would consider this a dead end, but Barrus was no quitter. He invented the pen name Nasdijj, which afforded him a Navajo identity and credibility in the eyes of Native American literary critics. Still faced with the dilemma of finding a Native American personal history to chronicle in his memoirs, he sought out other genuine experiences in the work of Native American authors such as Sherman Alexie and Leslie Silko, and he copied and pasted their writing into his books. His books were critically acclaimed for years before he was investigated and ultimately exposed as a fraud.

25. Embellish a Resumé

If things have gotten so sorry that you actually have to ask somebody for a job, then it's important to have a resumé. There is a great possibility that this interviewer is not even your intellectual equal, yet she is the one evaluating *you*. But after having to earn food money last week by hawking your favorite ass beads on Craigslist, you realize that you flat-out need the employment. With winning resumé-building tips like these, not only will you wow your interviewer, she may even let you sodomize her with her mouse.

Fact over Fiction

Resumé embellishment alters the subtleties and keeps the factual overtones intact. You do not want to outright lie on a resumé, because there are penalties for dishonesty, and there is no statute of limitations for resumé fraud. Well, maybe you can lie a little bit.

1. *Know what the prospective employer is seeking in an employee.* If you are going to perform, then you must understand your audience. There is no rule limiting people to one resumé at a time. If you are applying to three different employers, then research those companies, analyze the job descriptions, and modify your resumé accordingly for each separate company.

2. *Emphasize the skills that you have developed* in your professional past. While some of your previous jobs may not have had impressive titles, creative phrasing and a sprinkling of hyperbole may still impress the readers of your resumé. Gas station clerks are adept at customer service and facilitating financial exchanges.
3. *Include measurable accomplishments* in your job descriptions. When you explain your role in previous companies, you do not want to be too vague. Name a few specific examples of your handiwork. You may invent these facts, but most of us have a few shining moments to draw upon. Did you increase any company's revenue? Include a dollar amount. Did you win any awards? Did you have any commendations in your file for outstanding work? Did you do anything to improve the work atmosphere? Did you make any innovative contributions to the company's operations?
4. Build upon your *real* experience, and *avoid lame exaggerations.* Exaggerations work in moderation, but they become comical when they are overused. Do not exaggerate your job titles (secretaries are not chief administrative operators. Train-hopping hobos are not locomotive car inspectors); rather, draw attention to the duties that the jobs have entailed and the skills they have strengthened. Alter the subtleties.
5. *Use keywords*—but sparingly. A few keywords will capture the attention of the readers of your resumé, and they are advantageous when you submit an electronic application. However, too many keywords will make the resume seem robotic.

For a comprehensive list of excellent keywords, please visit resume-builder.org. There you'll find doozies such as:

Keywords from A to Z

advised
budgeted
cataloged
developed
extrapolated
facilitated
guided
headed

25. Build your resumé with creative phrasing. You weren't merely a cashier at the mall; rather you "facilitated financial exchanges for a Fortune 500 department store."

illuminated
judged
launched
moderated
nurtured
orchestrated
procured
quantified
resolved
safeguarded
transacted
transferred
undertook
verified
witnessed
zoned

Tips

1. *Artfully phrase* your education history. If you took a few courses but never graduated, then focus on the subject of study instead of the degrees earned. Internships and apprenticeships are loose terms, so squeeze a few of those into your history. Do you have any vocational training? Did you take any advanced courses in high school or college that you can call your "concentration"?
2. *Give yourself a well-rounded persona.* Have you ever volunteered (for just a few hours) or been affiliated with a charitable organization (even on the receiving end)? This can be included in a "community service" segment. This area consists of the names of organizations and the capacity within which you worked. That's it.
3. *Do not omit anything* that would throw the chronology of the resumé off kilter. If you were out of work for a year or two, then explain the absence. Did you take any courses during this "training period"?

FELON'S SECTION

26. Join the Mafia

If you are a violent person, then finding employment in the mafia can be a rewarding and lucrative career path. You don't need much education, you make good cash, you get to wear a gold pinky ring (yet still garner respect), and all you have to do is maim or kill, which you love! Mob guys eat great food for free, they get custom suits, the best seats, plus you get a stable of skanky goumadas. Instead of clocking into a menial job or doing the 9 to 5 in a lame office, you get to work at strip joints and look at tits all day. You're an important guy—you get to go on expense-paid road trips and give "urgent" messages to business associates. Like a doctor, you are entrusted to make life and death decisions while on the job. You get to see what people say and how they act just before they die—very fascinating, and very unique to your position. You get to stuff terrified people into trunks then drive around with your pals, going over speed bumps and laughing. There's also great exercise—digging shallow graves strengthens your biceps, triceps, and traps. You get to learn and enact awesome murder techniques like how to kill execution style, the art of the pick axe, or how to dump a live body in a vat of acid without any spillage. And if you're lucky enough to stay in the business long enough, you're given the job security of a Supreme Court judge.

Networking

Mob membership is premised on networking and promotion from within. You must know a member of the Mafia, or a soldier, before you start thinking about induction. Figure out what you can offer the Mafia before you inquire about membership. If you are just a punk with no skills, then you may be

26. Performing a quality murder is a smart way to earn acceptance from your peers. For a quick and silent killing, approach the goombah from the rear, grasp his mouth and nose in a clamped palm, and simultaneously thrust the knife into the right kidney area.

used for a few jobs and forgotten, or worse. You need to master a specific niche that will increase the mafia's revenue. Are you a brilliant computer hacker? Do you have legal expertise? Are you a skilled fighter? An expert in weaponry? A crafty businessman? The owner of a business that may share a symbiotic relationship with the mob? An experienced con man, forger, money launderer, or burglar? Figure out your angle and promote yourself to your connection.

Inform that member that you are interested in becoming an associate or soldier, and see what happens. If you are considered for recruitment, then you will likely be given an initiation assignment or series of assignments. If you perform your tasks with satisfactory results, you will be an associate for a prolonged period of time to gauge your loyalty, your competence, and your character. You will not become a member of the Mafia immediately. Some people work for the mob and never become members.

Be Cool

Maintain a close, respectful relationship with your superiors while you are working as a recruit, and make sure that they know your aspirations to become a member. Never pester them about your membership, just keep up a casual rapport with them and let them draw conclusions about your future with the organization.

Now Prove It

While you are a recruit, you may be asked to commit heinous crimes that have no relevance to your realm of expertise. A prospective Mafioso is carefully supervised and tested to assess his obedience, discretion, ability, and ruthlessness. He is almost always required to commit murder as his ultimate trial. Many recruits die or go to jail before they are inducted.

Prison

You may also become a recruit in prison. The Mafia's territory encompasses the prisons in which its leaders are incarcerated. Develop a relationship with an associate or a boss in prison, and perform any tasks assigned to you, and you may be on your way to induction.

LEGENDS OF BAD

Richard Kuklinski

In any job interview, it's essential to make a quality first impression. In his Mafia audition, Richard Kuklinski truly shined. Conducting Kuklinski's job interview from inside a car that was idling on a city street, Gambino mobster Roy DeMeo pointed to a random man walking his dog on the sidewalk and challenged Kuklinski to kill him. Without questioning it, Kuklinski went up and shot the guy in the back of the head—and a stellar career was born. Kuklinski carried out hundreds of mob-ordered executions. He was a creative master, using a multitude of murder techniques: guns, knives, strangulation, cyanide, and Kuklinski's particular favorite, hiding victims in secluded caves and using rats to eat them alive. To avoid capture, Kuklinski killed almost every friend he had ever known. After a lucrative, thirty-year career he was finally captured—turned in by the one friend he didn't kill.

27. Smuggle Materials

There are few experiences more rewarding than traveling the world and immersing yourself in foreign cultures. If you are not a particularly wealthy individual, or you haven't won a game show prize, a good way to arrange a trip abroad, to say Brazil, Thailand or Jamaica, is to befriend a smuggler and then do him a favor. Learning how to properly smuggle is an invaluable talent that everybody should learn.

Perhaps you've been living abroad, teaching remedial English to locals, and then you get fired for some minor infraction, say fondling your favorite student. Still, you want to extend your stay abroad. Smuggling can help you here.

It's also important to know how to properly smuggle, in case you've had a lapse of judgment and you're already in too deep to get out. Maybe you've been hanging out in Argentina and you've just smoked some hashish with a stranger, and the drug temporarily changes your mood and behavior, and logic—and the next thing you know you've agreed to smuggle a few kilos to Denver as a way of saying thank you.

You can smuggle materials in your body, on your body, or in a vessel. Remember to always smuggle a little at a time. Carrying huge quantities of goods will make you conspicuous, and you will be stopped by the police.

The Statue Method

Buy a souvenir statue, cut open the bottom, and fill it with the material to be smuggled. Use glue or putty to reseal the statue and conceal the goods. You may just ship the statue to the address of the intended recipient of the materials (or to the address of a medium who will then sell the goods to many recipients). You may also place the statue in a duffel bag with clothing and other souvenirs, and you may check the bag at the airport before you board the plane.

Figure 27. Choose an inconspicuous statue with a weighty base and carefully break it apart . . .

Figure 28. Place the tightly wrapped materials inside . . .

Figure 29. Reseal with matching glue or putty.

Foodstuffs

Separate the materials and hide small quantities in packages containing food. If it is a powdery substance, then sprinkle some powder into the bottom of a Cheez-it box, leaving the bag of Cheez-its full, but open, above. Separate the powder into small bags, and insert each bag between Pringle chips, then place the bags and Pringles back in the container, or insert the materials inside the core of a fruit. Do not take the opened food through security checks at airports or any other check-point that will require you to empty the food and liquid from your containers. Pack the food into a bag that you will check at the airport.

Other Methods

In aspirin. Encase powdery substance to make it look like over-the-counter tablets. Keep them in a bottle bearing the same name as the tablets.

Your body. Strapping the materials to your body is a risk, but you may surgically implant them in your thigh. (Using animals is a popular, and, some would say, inhumane method.)

Plexiglas. Insert liquid materials into Plexiglas and then use the glass to build an object that you can carry with you or ship to another destination.

By car

- If you are trafficking goods by car, then *travel with an animal.* If a drug official pulls you over, the drug dog will be distracted by your animal, and he may miss the stash.
- *Travel in the rain,* because there may be fewer officials on the road.
- *Drive during rush hour,* and blend into the traffic. Do not tote anything that may attract attention to your car.
- If you are trafficking the goods in a truck, then *hide the materials* under the floorboards, and pack the truck with something uninviting for inspectors: Snakes, bears, a ton of manure, or anything along these lines may work.

Higher budgets will allow you to use a semisubmersible vessel to transport the materials just below the ocean's surface. This is feasible only if you have made a lucrative career in trafficking.

28. Make Counterfeit Money

There's nothing more American than *making* money. And sometimes, due to financial shortfalls or injustices, it pays to make your own. Say you've been pouring thousands of dollars into local school taxes every year, yet you have no children of your own. Why should you pay to educate somebody else's brat—possibly with an annoying name like Micah or Riley—and get nothing for it? What about all that dough you've been forced to donate into Social Security? Doesn't look like a strong return on investment will be coming your way. For these reasons, and countless others, "currency creation" is almost justifiable. Better yet, according to a certain United States Federal Reserve chairman, it is actually good for the economy during a liquidation crisis. The government is giving trillions of our dollars to banks, yet the banks are too fearful to lend it. If your high-quality fakes enter the circulation, you are helping to spark American commerce and can help prevent a depression. You can be a patriot!

What's great is that you no longer have to be a skilled technician with a basement full of offset printers to churn out your $10's, $20's, and $50's. Today, to be a master of money, all you need is everyday modern technology and a little ingenuity. Here are two techniques with which to start making your own money.

The "Washing Washington" Method

People sometimes get detected because the paper doesn't match a true cash bill or the currency fails modern detection tests such as the detection pen or a lack of watermarks. The "*Washing Washington*" method helps you wipe away suspicion and bypass these potential threats. Don't think of it as counterfeiting; think of it as an art project.

You will need the following objects and ingredients:

Iron and ironing board
Bleach
Acetone
Hydrogen peroxide (3 percent)
Measuring cup (ml)
Bowl
$1 bills (more bills equals more money)
Rubber gloves
Protective mask
Kleenex
Level countertop
Envelopes (size #10)
Weighty book (dictionary)
Computer image of 1968 U.S. dollar bill (front and back), the value of which you want to duplicate. ($5, $10, or $20 recommended to avoid suspicion.)
Scanner/Printer

Phase 1: Preparation

1. *Iron your $1 bills until they are flat and crisp.* Make sure your bills have no flaws or rips. Only use bills that are in perfect condition.
2. *Pour 500 ml of bleach into bowl.*
3. *Pour 500 ml of acetone into bowl.*

30. Make your new money with these common household items.

4. *Pour 500 ml of hydrogen peroxide into bowl.* You'll notice a bubbling, hot chemical reaction. This elixir melts away the ink on the currency.
5. *Put on your rubber gloves and mask.* Inhaling the chemical smell can be toxic.

Phase 2: "Washing" Your Currency

1. *Soak $1 bill in chemical bowl* for ten minutes.
2. *Lay bill on countertop.*
3. Use the Kleenex tissue, and in a circular motion, *carefully wipe away ink from the front of the $1 bill.* You will need to repeat this step an additional three or four times—only soaking for two minutes—to remove all of the ink. When you are done the front of the bill will appear blank and white or pearl in color.

4. Run the entire $1 bill beneath a slow stream of hot water to *remove excess chemicals.*
5. *Repeat step 4* under cold water.

   (Note: If the money tears it will further deteriorate and cannot be used, and you must begin again.)
6. *Put $1 bill inside the envelope* and place the weighty book on top to flatten.
7. Wait ninety minutes so it can harden and regain its natural form.

   (Note: Examine your $1 bill. Its texture should feel unchanged. The front should be blank, but the back should still appear normal. You may also see small droplets of ink, which is normal.)
8. Delicately *re-iron the $1 bill* to remove or suppress the remaining ink droplets.
9. *Repeat steps 1–8* for the back of the bill. When you have finished you will have an entirely blank $1 bill. How much cash do you want to print? Do the same process for all additional $1 bills.

Phase 3: Printing Your Cash

1. *Scan, in high resolution,* the front and back of the 1968 currency, in the monetary amount you have chosen. U.S. currency from 1968 and prior are still in circulation, yet have none of the security features that are used today, such as watermarks and counterfeit detection pens sensitive to paper.

   (Note: You may also scan in more recent bills. But they have security features and you must hope you don't run into a vigilant money checker. Though most people don't inspect currency closely, for this reason, it is recommended that you at first stake out the place you'll be cashing in your new currency to ensure that you find a person who won't cause you problems. To be safe, this holds true if you are using the 1968 currency as well.)

2. *Print (using colored ink)* the front of the scanned 1968 currency onto one side of your blank $1 bill.
3. *Print the back* of the scanned 1968 currency onto the other side of your blank $1 bill.
4. *Wait sixty minutes* for ink to dry.
5. *Re-iron* your new money. You're good to go!

The "Cutting Corners" Method

This is one of the quickest, simplest forms of counterfeiting. And it feels just like real paper money, because it is. Because most people don't analyze cash closely, this is often an effective method.

You will need the following:

Four $20 bills
Four $1 bills
Superglue

1. *Cut four different corners* from four $20 bills. (Even though one corner is removed, this currency will still be accepted.)
2. *Glue* them in place over the corners of $1 bills.

Blank Checking

If you're not happy with the dollar amount of a check written to you, simply change it. It's easy. Just use the same chemical solution for the "Washing Washington" technique.

You will need the following:

Bleach
Acetone
Hydrogen peroxide

Bowl
Cotton ball
A check written out to you
Flat, hard countertop

1. *Pour* 500 ml of bleach into bowl.
2. *Pour* 500 ml of acetone into bowl.
3. *Pour* 50 ml of hydrogen peroxide into bowl.
4. *Soak* half of a cotton ball in the chemical solution.
5. Using the cotton ball, *lightly rub* away the dollar amount written in ink. Leave the date, signature, and your name intact.

Write in the new dollar amount of your choice.

LEGENDS OF BAD

Mary Butterworth

Mary Butterworth was a colonial counterfeiter who found a way to combine her familial duties and her desire to be a career woman: she put the kids to work in a family counterfeiting plant. Between churning butter and burying victims of yellow fever, Mary Butterworth ran a counterfeiting operation with a turnout so prolific that it compromised the colonial economy. Her methodology included lifting ink from bills with damp cotton, stamping the pattern impression on new bills using a hot iron press, and using a quill to fill in the ink by hand. Authorities closed in on Butterworth after her husband made a few extravagant purchases, and many of her family members, including her brother, were pressured into testifying against her during the trial. Despite the testimonies, Butterworth's case was dismissed and she either abandoned her counterfeiting enterprise or tightened her control of her husband's spending habits, because she was never caught again.

29. Grow Marijuana

Growing and smoking your own marijuana means you don't have to spend money supporting the illegal deeds of pot dealers, and instead you can spend your money supporting coke dealers. Their gangs in Mexico need weaponry, plus there's the expense of having to hire hitmen and bribing government officials, all of which costs a bundle.

Or what if you're a cult leader in Humboldt County, California, you're known as the Messiah, the sex is amazing, and the only way you can continue to fund the lifestyle is by growing fields of cannabis below the government's radar.

Or you could be a broke college student, and with the skyrocketing costs of pot, you can't even afford textbooks. It'd be a shame to have to drop out of school when you can learn how to grow your own.

1. *Extract the seeds* from a clump of marijuana (or use a cutting from another female plant—do not use a cutting from a male plant. (If you use a cutting, your harvest will take about a week longer than the seed grown plants.)
2. To be certain that the seeds will yield plants, you may want to *germinate* them by placing them in a moist paper towel until they begin to crack (this process may take one day or one week).

3. *Find an indoor location* that is both well lit and private. You may want to line the walls with tinfoil, white plastic, or paint them matte white to reflect the sun's glare onto the plants. A room with a window will provide adequate light, but if there are no private windowed rooms, then a closet, pantry, or dry basement is the next best thing. You will need plenty of lamps to compensate for lack of sunlight. Position one or two lamps (preferably fluorescent heat lamps) about two or three inches away from each planter. Keep a fan running at all times in this room.
4. *Choose a relatively small container* (between 4-6 inches in diameter), and fill it with topsoil. Prepare the soil by watering it and tilling it. Make sure that it drains well when you water it. If it does not seem to drain well, you should go to a local nursery and ask for well-draining, low-acid soil.
5. *Spread a few seeds* into your container, and then sprinkle dirt on top of the seeds. Water 2-3 times daily.
6. Keep the lamps about two inches from each marijuana plant, and reposition the lamps as the plants grow. Remember to *give the plants a twelve-hour dark period every day.* When the lights are off in the room, the room should be in total darkness.
7. Gradually begin to *fertilize your plants* between harvestings. You do not want to feed your plants fertilizer right before a harvest because it will cause heavy foliage and scant resin production. Limit their consumption of water for the last two weeks before harvest.
8. Always *watch the acid levels in the soil.* To avoid heavy salt or acid accumulation in the soil, you can leaf feed your plants by fertilizing the leaves directly with a di-

luted spray solution. The pH of the soil should remain between 5 and 6.

9. *Keep the room ventilated.* A fan will suffice in a smaller space, but you may need a more elaborate exhaust system in a larger room.
10. *The plants will take about 8–12 weeks to harvest.* You can tell that your plant is about to harvest when most of the stigmas, or the hairs sticking out of the buds, shrivel and turn brown. You may also look at the THC glands with a magnifying glass. When they are milky white, they are ripe and the buds are at their peak.

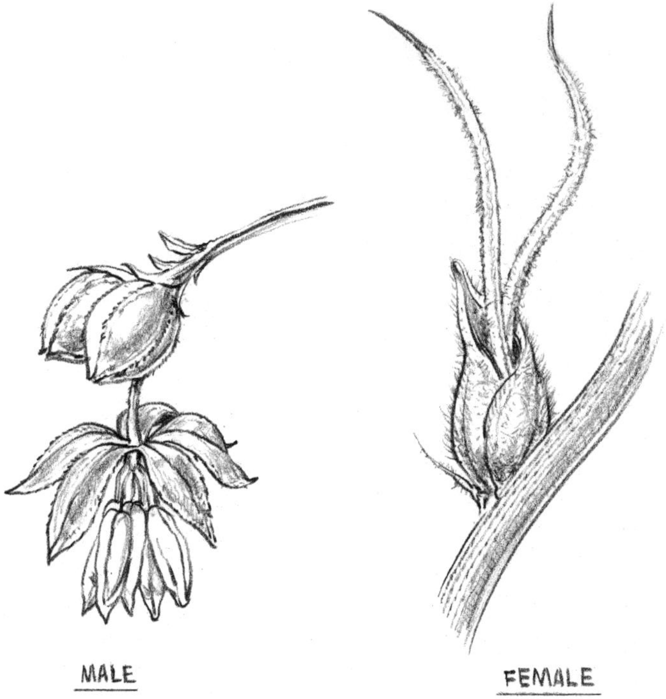

31. To get the ball rolling, begin with seeds or the cuttings from a female plant.

11. Once you have trimmed the cannabis colas, *you need to dry the leaves.* The drying space needs to be room temperature, ventilated, and dark.
12. *Check your plant for mold*—if you find any, trim the moldy pieces from the rest so that they don't contaminate anything.
13. To *dry the cannabis,* hang it from a string to drain the water from the stems and leaves. Dry cannabis is firm, but not brittle. Once they are dry, store them in dark, airtight containers.
14. The plants will grow quickly, so be ready to transplant them to larger containers. After a few weeks, you should transplant them to three-gallon containers. To *transplant a marijuana plant,* simply turn the existing container upside-down, pat the bottom of the container to loosen the soil and dislodge the root ball, and gently place the root ball into a root-ball-sized hole in the soil of the new container.

Keep It Going

Cut portions of the plant and transplant them to new containers to form new plants. Make sure that you cut enough hard stem at a 45-degree angle. If you notice male cannabis plants entering your selection, get rid of them. You do not want them germinating the female plants.

30. Rob a Bank

Baby Face Nelson, Bonnie and Clyde, Jessie James, D.B. Cooper. Look how respected these people are. That could be you. Even if you've traumatized a bank teller or some weak-minded bank customers, you have actually given them a chance to harden and learn how to overcome obstacles.

Few people can successfully rob a bank and escape with the money, and the ones who succeed often use the same formulas as the ones who fail. Chance and wily improvisation will certainly help determine the outcome of your bank job. Use this information to help you "get away" with it.

Inside Job

1. *Assemble a team.* You need to start with a powerful inside connection who can tell you the guard schedule, the police rotation, whether the guards are armed, and provide access to the drawers or the safe. Walking into a bank and demanding money from strangers is dangerous. If you have an inside man, he can take you to the safe as though you are performing a typical transaction, and when he hands over the money, you will leave as though you are a typical customer without arousing the suspicion of the employees or the customers. You also need a getaway driver.

2. Trust and loyalty will be the adhesive that keeps your crew together. *If you are suspicious of your crew, or you don't feel comfortable performing the job with them, then trust your intuition* and cancel the job. The tiniest flaw in your team can make you vulnerable.
3. *Case the bank and formulate a plan.* Do you want to take a small amount of money from the drawer or do you want to score a major sum from the safe? You need to know exactly how much you want, where you will obtain it, and how you will walk out with it. You need to construct a story before you go in. Who are you, and why do you need to see your inside connection (the bank employee) in his office? Why does he need to bring you to the safe to see your possessions or money? Rehearse it numerous times before the big day.
4. *Arrange escape plans.* Book a flight or plan a drive out of the country during the hours immediately following the job. The inside connection should meet you and the getaway driver about an hour after the job so as not to alert his coworkers. His departure from work should be planned ahead of time and approved by his boss (or acknowledged by his coworkers). If he actually travels out of the country in a separate vehicle, then it will be even more difficult to apprehend the full team en route to the destination.
5. *The job should be done during the bank's slow hours.* Your inside connection will outline the timeframe because he will be most familiar with his bank's business.
6. On the day of the job, *avoid drinking coffee or soda,* and maintain your equanimity when you walk in there. Believe your lie, and do not stray from the plan.

32. Aim to shoot below the waist. It could mean the difference between attempted murder and mere assault.

The Walk-Up Robbery

1. If you cannot pull off a discrete and classy robbery with an influential inside connection, then you need to arrange something more risky. You still need to assemble

a team, case the bank, know the guards, know the police rotation, locate the drawers and safes, and *establish an inside link.* The actual sequence of the job will differ, though.

2. *Plan your strategy for weeks or months* leading up to the big day, and make sure every member of the team knows his or her responsibilities. Map out your route from the bank door to the drawer or safe and back to the getaway car. The job should take no longer than thirty seconds.
3. *Use a getaway car* that has no obvious connections to anyone in your crew, and stash a second getaway car and a change of clothes in a garage a few miles from the bank. This will be your immediate destination, granted you do not have to deal with a police chase.
4. On the day of the heist, *walk into the bank with a mask and a suit (and a gun if you need one).* The getaway driver should be circling the block, and you should have some communication method to inform him of the exact moment that he is needed in front of the bank.
5. *Inform the employees that this is a robbery,* and approach the drawers and safe with *your own bags* to fill with money. Do not take a bag provided by the bank, because they will be rigged. Stuff money into the bags quickly, and never lose sight of the time. If you get too greedy, then you will spend too much time in the bank and you will risk being caught by the police.
6. If you are involved in a shootout, *do not shoot anyone above the waist,* because that becomes an attempted murder charge. Aiming below the waist is usually only considered assault.
7. *The getaway driver needs to have flawless timing* (either due to your cue or the pre-planned synchronization).

Drive to the garage harboring the second car, ditch the getaway car, change your clothes, and resume your lives. You will want to destroy the getaway car later by burning it or driving it into a lake. Make sure you leave no forensic evidence linking you to that car.

8. *Launder the money.* If you plan to continue living normally, then you need to launder and exchange the money to cover your tracks. Do not go on shopping binges or do anything out of the ordinary.
9. If you plan to leave the country and begin a new life with your cash, then do so immediately. *Do not stick around to say goodbye to loved ones,* because some people will start to connect the bank robbery to your departure. You may want to fake your own death before you leave.

31. Commit Bigamy

They say being a family man is a dignified thing. So if you have a couple of families, you must be quite upstanding. For some men it is probably hard to fathom why one would actively seek to double or triple the aggravations and irritations that come with having a family. To cope with the stress, if you become a religious fundamentalist, with ten or twelve wives, you can batter a different wife every day for a few weeks. This will keep your relationships exciting. As for the children, you'll probably get an accurate read on which spouse breeds the uglier or more annoying offspring, and that way you can limit these rejects to a minimum of one child.

Mormons and Muslims

Polygamy is practiced by a number of cultures on religious grounds. Many fundamentalist Mormons and Muslims marry two or more wives, so if you are already connected to a church or mosque that performs such ceremonies, then the process is easy. Otherwise, try to find a link to an institution that will perform a second or third marriage (Islam does not approve of more than four wives at a time).

33. Having an additional wife to batter can be a cathartic release.

Marry in Different Countries

- *Marry each wife in a different country.* Go on a continental drive and marry a whore in Tijuana, a golddigger in New Jersey, and a bobsledder in Alberta. Just go to local chapels or marriage offices that do not have access to global files.

32. Commit Insider Trading

Insider trading obtains information from nonpublic sources, such as family, friends, or business contacts, to profit in the financial market. It is difficult to prove that someone is guilty of insider trading, so the best technique is to avoid providing the prosecutor with evidence that you had any definitive knowledge before you bought or sold.

It's Not Unethical

Acting on information one has obtained from nonpublic sources is actually employing smart business acumen, and should not be punished, as long as one is not in violation of the rights of others. If one has honestly obtained information ahead of another player in the trading community, they are just being prudent. The beaten player, therefore, should not automatically have a right to this information. Say you happen upon solid information with due diligence—for example, you overhear a couple of corporate blowhards discussing company numbers at the urinals, while you're puking out tequila in the bathroom stall. You shouldn't be obligated to inform your financial competition of this information simply because you have expertly placed yourself in the right place at the right time.

Take a Hit

If you hear news that would suggest that a company's stocks will plummet overnight, sell *many, but not all* stocks with that company. Sell additional stock that is completely unrelated to this deal.

33. Assume Somebody's Identity

Once you've stolen the ID of a long-dead infant, a fun thing to do is approach the family and tell them that you were buried alive, and that you never actually died because you were able to gnaw out of your tomb. You've spent years getting back your physical and emotional strength, and finally, you have let the anger and hurt subside, and you are ready to reconnect. If your new parents don't believe you, show them your ID and tell them the details of the death, which you read all about in the obituary. Or you might want to wait to reach out to them until they are elderly and senile enough so that they can leave you your rightful inheritance.

There are two types of Identity Theft victims: the living and the dead.

Assuming a Dead Person's ID

1. To adopt the identity of a dead man, you must first *find that winning corpse*. The ideal identity will be someone who was born during your birth year and died during infancy or childhood. You can find the right match by perusing graveyards or obituary archives.
2. Once you figure out who you want to become, *order his or her birth certificate* from its issuing source. You can explain that you lost the birth certificate, you are a rela-

tive composing a genealogy chart, your current birth certificate is too worn or damaged, and so on.

- *Create a fraudulent birth certificate.* Take your real birth certificate, make a photocopy, omit your personal information from that copy, make a copy of the blank certificate, fill in the dead man's identity on the blank copy, and make a final copy that will prominently display the new information. Artificially age the birth certificate by submerging it in a tea solution, leaving it in the sun, and folding and refolding it until it appears weathered.

3. *Get the social security card*: You may either apply for a social security number (you will need to explain why you have not bothered to apply for a number until now, and you may be rejected by an office or two, but keep persisting in different offices until someone prints out a card for you), or you may invent a social security number. The first three numbers are paramount, because they must correspond with the official code of the issuing state. The second two numbers indicate the original date of issuance, and the last four numbers represent the sequence of offices used to sign up your identity, and it is difficult to verify the validity of any sequence.
4. *Go to the D.M.V.* of a lenient state, and file for a driver's license.
5. *Create a bank account online,* and try to avoid spending too much time in the bank. Use the ATM and online banking options.
6. Respond to a few credit card offers, and begin to *establish your lines of credit.*

34. Surprise your new "parents" by assuming the identity of their long-dead infant.

Assuming a Living Person's ID

This only explains how to steal someone's identity *without* the use of software programs or scanners. The hands-on way to start would be to actually steal a credit card. Otherwise, you could rifle through the trash in a foreign neighborhood, and steal any bank statements, credit card statements, credit card offers, pay stubs, credit card carbons, and tax documents you can find. If you can find numerous documents that disclose personal information about the same person, then that is your victim.

1. If you are just looking for a free credit card to use, then *look for the information that Web sites require.* Name, address, account number, expiration date, and security code are pretty standard. If you have access to that information, then you have a new line of credit.

2. Use the information on the documents to *look up a person's credit report.* Once you obtain the credit report, you have enough personal information to begin establishing yourself as this person's digital doppelganger. Disguise yourself as this person by using their information and their passwords online. You may change their passwords by accessing their accounts, using the password reset feature, then accessing their e-mail to finish the job. You must obviously find this information on the credit report or in the discarded documents in the trash in order to perform this task. Do not frequent Web sites, do not use your own computer (use public computers, and do not return to the scene of the crime), and never use the information in person.

3. *Use the person's existing account* to fund your online spending *or* open additional credit accounts in this person's name.

Work as an operator for a financial institution. People need to divulge personal information to you, so record this information and use it to create aliases and spending accounts online.

34. Escape Prison

You've been wrongly incarcerated, at least by *your own* moral standard of what is right and what is wrong, and now you have to find a way to escape from prison. Yes, perhaps you *did* kill your next-door neighbor, you can admit to that. But he was constantly complaining to you about the loudness of your Harley choppers. Sure, sometimes you and your pals—all decent, violent people—would rev up the choppers and head to the strip club—but you *never* came home after 4 A.M., *never.* Plus you *only* went Mondays through Thursdays. Then one day you're taking your mid-afternoon nap, when suddenly you're rudely awakened by a policeman at the door. He writes you a citation for disturbing the peace. After the cop leaves, you do what comes naturally, and hop over your neighbor's fence and bludgeon him to death with his own claw hammer. Obviously, what happened to your neighbor was entirely his fault—yet *you* are the one being incarcerated. And, if he hadn't indirectly woken you up from your deep sleep, then perhaps you would have been thinking more clearly, and his life could have been saved. If your situation is similar to this, and you are in fact, wrongly incarcerated, this is all of the moral standing that you need to justify breaking out of prison and breaking the law—even if you must kill a female guard or two in the process. Follow these steps and get your freedom back.

Inside Job

The most effective prison breaks involve inside men (guards or prison administrative officials). So you need to provide a product or service to those influential figures at the very beginning of your prison term. Once you have established a working relationship and a rapport with certain staff members, determine which ones seem susceptible to bribery.

Once you have found your man, start the manipulation game. Analyze his character to figure out whether he is more responsive to threats, promises of power, or friendship. When you are confident that you have figured out his triggers, start molding him.

- *Persuade him to reduce your security level.* If you are reduced to minimum security, then you will be allowed more visitors, and you will be under less surveillance.
- If you are granted more visitors under limited surveillance, then you can begin *plotting your escape with the visitors*. Have them map out an escape route from the prison wall to a destination safely out of reach of the guards in the tower.
- *Recruit an accomplice* from the outside to actually navigate the route and figure out where treachery lies and what materials are necessary to aid the escape.
- *The accomplice must supply those materials* by hiding them in locations agreed upon by yourself and him on the day of the escape.
- *Plot your route to the edge of the prison grounds.* (You must know all of the pitfalls of the property: Consider the guards' vantage point, figure out your wall-climbing strategy, and determine the exact amount of time you will need.) Do not inform anybody of your plans, and do not behave suspiciously while you map your route.

Make mental notes, because written notes will be discovered. Persuade your inside connection to assign you to lawn maintenance or any task that will place you in an advantageous location (do not disclose your plans to your inside connection).

- If all goes well, you will have a clear path to the wall on the day of the escape. *Make sure that nobody is watching you too closely,* and create a diversion (if possible) right before the break. While the guards are distracted, calmly make your way out of sight, and execute your escape plan.

One-Man Job

It is not always possible to make guards swoon for you, so if you cannot forge an inside connection, then you will have to coordinate the job on your own, or with the help of another inmate.

- *You still need an outside connection* to plot the route from the prison grounds to a safer destination in the distance (and to provide the necessary materials to aid the escape). Without that information, it will be difficult to find your way back to freedom.
- *Chart the ventilation systems,* the sewage system—any pipes or ducts large enough to accommodate a slithering human body. Identify the connective points, the passage openings, the composition of the material (what kind of tools need to penetrate it?), and the locations of the external outlets or openings.
- *Create or obtain tools that will allow you to dig a channel* connecting to the closest plumbing or ventilation passageway. Begin digging surreptitiously, and set a deadline for reaching the escape path. You will need a decoy

vent, poster, or wall covering to place over the digging site.

- Once you make it to the escape passageway, move quickly, follow your plans carefully, and be vigilant.

Additional Methods

- If you have numerous visitors, then you may use the lenient visiting forum to your advantage. Have visitors go into the visitors' bathroom and *hide one article of clothing at a time* for you to retrieve (or you could just do it all in one shot). When you have a full ensemble to don, change into the civilian clothes, and exit the prison as a civilian.
- You could use the above technique with laundry supplies, as well. *Find a way to work in the laundry room,* and, as soon as you have access to a military uniform or a set of civilian clothes, you can walk out in disguise.
- *Hide inside of garbage trucks or food delivery trucks* that work the prison route.
- *Seduce a guard,* and take advantage of his or her vulnerability. Coax him into aiding your escape, or disarm him, disrobe him, and keep him restrained while you walk out of the prison in his uniform.
- *Escape in numbers.* If three or four inmates (all of whom are trustworthy) are running from prison in different directions, then it is more difficult to track them down.
- *Use ingenuity, patience, and persistence.* Use prison-issued floss to cut through bars, use prison work-release programs to open up conduits between you and the free world, develop connections in prison that may abet the process, and so on.

35. Use your prison-issued floss, and dogged persistence, to methodically cut through the steel bars.

LEGENDS OF BAD

Pascal Payet

Pascal Payet was a man who had no patience for discretion or clandestine strategy. After he was imprisoned for the murder of a driver during a security van robbery, he plotted the only practical means of escape from his French prison cell: hijacking a helicopter to land on the roof of the prison and fly him to freedom. Foolproof. The technique worked so well that he later used it to aid the escape of friends in Luynes prison and to aid his second escape from prison after he was recaptured by authorities.